POCKET GUIDE TO YOUR HEART FOR RELATIONSHIPS

POCKET GUIDE TO YOUR HEART FOR RELATIONSHIPS

Become the Beloved
to Attract and Inspire
the Beloved Relationship

by

Colleen Hoffman Smith

Heart Bridge Publishing
Toronto Canada

Published in 2005 by Heart Bridge Publishing
P.O. Box 67063, South Common PO,
Mississauga, Ontario, Canada L5L 5V4

www.pocketguidetoyourheart.com

Library and Archives Canada Cataloguing in Publication

Smith, Colleen Hoffman, 1953-
Pocket guide to your heart for Relationships :
become the beloved to attract and inspire the beloved relationship
/ by Colleen Hoffman Smith.

Includes bibliographical references.
ISBN 0-9734020-1-6

1. Love. 2. Man-woman relationships. I. Title.

BF575.I5S62 2005 158.2 C2004-907057-6

Cover and illustrations: Nancy Newman
Cover photo: Yanka and Henk Van der Kolk
Imaging and Photography
Print and production management: Karen Petherick,
Intuitive Design International Ltd.

Printed and Bound in Canada

DEDICATED TO

My Beloved Husband Bruce
I appreciate every moment
In your arms of safe love
We dance so well together
I Am In Love
With You

CONTENTS

ACKNOWLEDGEMENTS

I acknowledge with deep gratitude and love:

My wonderful daughters Lindsay, Lauren and my step-daughter Jessica for all the joy I feel with your precious smiles and loving hearts.

My parents Phil and Sue Hoffman and Bob and Joan Smith for always supporting my dreams with love.

My sisters and brothers Frannie and Steve, Philomene and Ray, Philip and Janine, Dave and Noelle, Stu and Helen who continue to inspire me about the journey of partnership and the importance of family.

To all of my nieces and nephews that show me freedom as you dance with your spirit and explore the freedom of your heart.... Luke, Lane, Jessie Meaghan, Bronwyn, Sarah, Michelle and Kevin.

Jo-Anne Cutler you are an awesome friend and exceptional manager. Thank you for being the mid-wife to this book, I could not have done it without you. Your support reminds me each day how important our message is.

Nancy Newman...Wow! You did it again.
Your illustrations and artistry give my words
life and feelings. You are fantastic.

Bettina Mann your friendship and desk top expertise
continue to assist me with each project.
You are great!

Karen Petherick your creative design and talent
took my book carefully to the final stage
of edit and layout.

My Goddess girl-friends....
I always feel your unconditional loving connection.
Thank you for being so patient while I completed
this project. I love being in my playful heart
with you.

My many clients who are my friends encourage me
daily to continue to share my experiences and divine
truth. You inspire me!

PROLOGUE

My life experiences connecting me to my emotions are really no different than anyone else's, just dressed up in details unique to me. The process of experiencing all the parts of myself with another person has been my greatest gift. With each person in my life who has mirrored my light and love it has been an easy relationship. The tough ones, those that have reflected my lack of love, my fear, anger, separation and resentment, are the relationships that have taught me the most about myself. When I look back, I remember blaming and judging someone else or myself when I was unhappy, which was okay because this is where I had to be at the time. Sometimes we react and misbehave. Can we still love ourselves in this place?

The love and peace that I've found with another person, at times lifted the darkness that needed to be felt. But there were days I didn't understand why I felt so shut down when I was being loved.

As I sit and write about my relationships, I see that each one offered the opportunity to get to know myself more.

Taking responsibility for what I was feeling with another, not blaming anyone or holding onto resentment freed me from my uncomfortable self. Once I felt the truth of my suppressed feelings – and only when I forgave them and myself – I could then feel the openness of my heart and the love within.

Relationship becomes comfortable or uncomfortable and it is up to us to be conscious of how we feel.

The ideal relationship is first with ourselves – to be comfortable by creating the connection within. The intimacy with truth, the freedom of fear and the strength of self-love, are all powered by the inner connection to our own source, our life force – SELF-LOVE, SELF-WORTH and SELF-AWARENESS.

I believe that God and the universe make no mistakes when two people are brought together ... it's not an accident! When I changed my perception of another and saw the truth as it pertained to what I was feeling or what I needed to own, I didn't have to attract the same experience again. I saw that each person that made me feel uncomfortable was taking me to the place inside that was devoid of love.

The *Pocket Guide to your He♥rt* formula created the inner support to help me take care of my uncomfortable feelings. The **Inner Relationship** connects to my issues instead of attaching to everyone else's. The **Inner Workout** acts as a tool for me to practice letting go, as I surrender myself to the truth of my emotions, such as resentment, anger and fear, and release them from my body. Once I let go of this heaviness, I can reconnect with the love and **Inner Peace** that is waiting to be embraced.

There is a Zen story about a lion who was brought up by sheep and who thought he was a lamb, until the old lion took him to the pond where he showed him his own reflection. The image we have of ourselves is derived from the reflection of others. Our personality can be imposed on us by society, but our individuality comes from within. The lion within is the strength of our will, our spirit. The sheep personality can influence us or delay or stop our individuality. Self-discovery leads us to our truth and our desires, showing us our highest potential when we connect to all that we are. We must allow our outer world to be the reflection of who we are and who we are not.

The *Pocket Guide to your He♥rt* formula has been my connection to my Inner Relationship, Inner Workout and Inner Peace. This process continues to strengthen my awareness of my self-worth, allowing me to experience my life and each relationship with an open and loving heart. This book is the expression of my process and the formula that I use daily to connect to the beloved within and the way I attracted my beloved partner, Bruce. Our mirror reflection of each other ignites our world.

The *Pocket Guide to your He♥rt for Relationships* addresses many types of relationship and can guide you to explore the faces of truth through self-discovery. For example: "Why do I keep attracting the same hard lessons in relationship over and over again?"

Everyone is searching for or dreaming of their perfect partner. This guide is an opportunity to take you there and gives you the formula to keep you there ... in the Beloved Experience.

The *Pocket Guide to your He♥rt* practice created a fresh awareness within where I saw clearly how I reacted and what I felt in my past relationships. I could then freely choose to love my own life and that expression of myself became attractive.

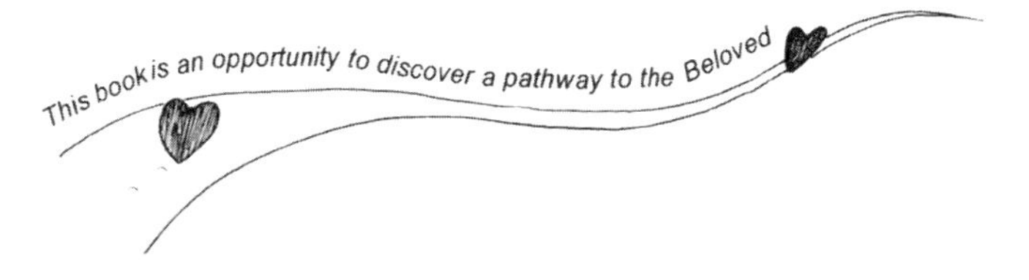

Today, as I remember my past, I feel the difference in my whole body. Who I was in relationship then is totally different than who I am now. I now see that I struggled because I was not living with the truth of who I really was. I blamed others for my unhappiness. I had become inauthentic over the years because I controlled my feelings and others in order to be comfortable. I controlled with love. I gave love to fill people up so that they would be happy and I withdrew love when I was hurt or things didn't go the way I wanted.

This dance of mine looked wonderful to others. I was so loving and generous that people could hardly believe I was real. I was popular and I used my looks and my need for love to open every door, to bring the attention or recognition that I craved. Yet I was always looking for more love and my desperation soon became intense and exhausting. My intention was never to hurt anyone but if I didn't get back the love, I would withdraw, shut down or leave the relationship.

My need for love attracted the kind of men who ended up controlling and manipulating me to fill their own void and lack of self-love. They too had suppressed the pain and anger that created barriers. They would project intensely or close their hearts so that neither of us could feel love. I blamed them and I'm sure they blamed me. We were unable to speak about it without blame and we would hurt one another with painful words or silence. We grew apart because there was no intimacy, joy or laughter between us and we were consumed by the uncomfortable emotions that we expressed from within. Whenever I didn't feel love from the man in my life, the experience would repeat itself.

What did I do wrong? ? ? ? ?

Shame

I felt like the bad girl
I plugged into their pain

I would try to fix them.
I would become the good little girl.

I would become inauthentic.
Sometimes they would respond because I would fill them up.

If they didn't respond
I would feel the
punishment.

I would then:

Shut d
O
W
N

Feel the resentment
I would resent
I would take on *their pain*

My heart would close 

I would then make them feel **GUILT**

I didn't feel love—I was unloved and unloveable

I would then **punish** them

I was unplugged—I felt empty of love

I felt FULL of uNcomfortable emotions that I

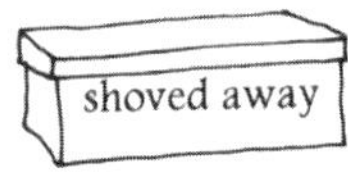

Every time that I felt
unloved and shut down
they would fill my ***void***
or they shut down
or they left ...

After three significant partnerships that attracted all of my greatest fears and made me physically ill, I realized that I had to live differently to truly live healthily and in peace. I can see the whole dance so clearly now because I understand how I behaved and why I reacted.

I found a way to let go of my resentment and unloving experiences. I created a process that would release the hurt and pain and fill me with love, creating a strong sense of self-worth.

I found peace and I became more authentic and attractive. This life process took me to a place within that allowed me to take responsibility, stop blaming men and forgive my past, so that I could live with an open heart.

THIS PLACE OF PEACE AND SELF-LOVE ATTRACTED MY BELOVED RELATIONSHIP

I'm going to share my intimate relationships with you as they happened when I took full responsibility for my choices. Each of these relationships enabled me to find out more about my inability to feel my own love. I lay no blame because I have worked hard at letting go of resentment. I am grateful for each experience and every moment of love or pain. Once I changed my perception, I could see the miracle in the relationship.

I could then LET GO!!!

I honor each significant partner that danced with me in the fire and abandoned me in the relationship. I forgive myself as I take responsibility for not being able to feel my own love at the same time they were feeling unloved or experiencing their own pain. We didn't know any other way to love ... and the world around us loved in the same way. Every significant relationship mirrored who I was at the time and each was a reflection of my own love and pain. I could only love as much as I knew how to feel love.

The love brought up the

PAIN

The light shone brightly on the

DARKNESS

Each relationship was a soul mate connection – each necessary for the evolution of my soul. Past relationships that still lived within me had shut down a part of my heart. I was so shut down and angry about a past partner that I forgot the love because I had not let go of the resentment and hurt.

Once I learned to let go, I had more space for love, because the love I felt for that person was my own love, not his ... I COULD THEN FEEL MORE OF MY OWN HEART. Instead of closing down my heart because a relationship reminded me of the void inside me, I learned to use the relationship to feel my pain and let go of the relationship. Once I released these suppressed emotions, I could re-connect with my own heart and source of love.

When you feel devastated by a failed relationship and you think that your heart is dead, you truly feel you will never find love again.

I remember the movie *Sleepless in Seattle* in which Tom Hanks said he couldn't grow a new heart. Dating is like trying someone on and seeing if they fit.

Take the time to heal your broken heart and find the love within so that you can attract a healthy, beautiful relationship. You will know inside when you are ready.

The *Pocket Guide to your He♥rt* formula can take you to a place:

- Of deep understanding of your emotions where you will find the freedom to be more present in your life
- To become more authentic and attractive in your present relationships
- To attract the beloved and enchanted relationship of love because you have embraced the beloved within
- To feel your own peace and love in relationship and partnership.

The "beloved" experience kicked in when I began to have a relationship with myself, when I found the understanding and truth within, and opened up to my own vastness. I could hear my soul's desires and find the wisdom to be all that I am in my heart.

My first two significant partners led me to struggle with myself and what the relationships reflected, took me to my truth. The loving connection with my inner child and the healing of hurt brought me to the awareness of my wounds. I could then experience and express "belovedness" and my next romance nourished the Goddess in me. Each level of trust guided me to more self-awareness, self-worth and many aspects of beloved love. I was ready for the beloved partnership when Bruce arrived.

You are the beloved and once you are comfortable with the pain and love inside, you can attract your reflection. When you are unaware of the love and peace within you, they can be like a foreign language; you may have no idea to what extent you are able to love or feel peace. You may not know because you haven't experienced it, or you may not even believe it's possible.

I had just finished reading *Enchanted Love* by Marianne Williamson when I met my beloved. I realized that this enchanted love was living in me. One of you may recognize the other … even in a busy airport!

By sharing my experiences with love and pain in relationship, I would like to show how my *Pocket Guide to your He♥rt* formula can help you sustain your strength and courage. It can also guide you past whatever is blocking the way, to open your heart and to create a safe place within where you can go to new places in a relationship – places where you fear the unknown, and where you can use this tool to help you release the pain of your damaged heart. To dance together differently and not hurt the other person in the process. You might feel the hurt, but this process will guide you past the pain to more love.

The Beloved Relationship can be a beautiful prayer.

Two hands touching ...

Intimately ... together.

Moving deeper inside relationship,

Falling in love ... deeper levels ...

Together ... deep love ...

Two hearts together ...

IN PRAYER

CHAPTER ONE

The Beloved Experience

The beloved is the experience of a safe rhythm of understanding and unconditional love between two hearts. In this place there is no judgment or expectation. The intention of love and peace, woven with respect, creates a safe place for each partner to become all that they are.

> *Darling, you want to know what I want of you. Many things of course, but chiefly these ... I want you to keep this thing we have, inviolate and waiting. The person who is neither I or you, but us.*
>
> John Steinbeck, American writer,
> to Gwendolyn, his wife – July 1943

It is in the design of the plan that two people come together when they are ready to evolve through their misery, understanding their soul's evolution, as they move through the darkness into a new sense of themselves in order to live the beloved experience. When you become connected to the beloved experience you can inspire another instead of taking the pathway outside yourself with blame. Become the beloved and inspire the beloved relationship, or attract the one who chooses to arrive at the same place.

The beloved experience is a vast space where we can heal ourselves. It's a place that is open and compassionate, where we can feel acknowledgement and understanding between ourselves and another. The gentle kindness creates a place of safety that is lifted within for two people, merging passion with endless love.

I asked my friend Ray, who continues to experience the beloved relationship with my sister, Philomene, what he felt. Ray is a writer and a spiritual intuitive and these are his words:

What I have learned is that Belovedness is seamless, like putting on a different sweater; the colors may be different and it has a different scent, but it fits perfectly, as though you had been wearing it all along. The mistake is to think that we become different in belovedness, rather than an enhanced version of who we essentially are. In the past, the energy of difference drove the initial passion, until the differences and conflicts of values drove the relationship into wounding because the partner wasn't the beloved. In the beloved, the energy of the divine becomes manifest in the love and passion of the bodies as well as the minds and emotions. The passion of loving is the energy of divine incarnate ... simply the energy of healing. Eastern religions have known this for some time. Belovedness is the experience of a deep and profound peace where the stillness is only interrupted by your inner smile.

Ray Imai, 2004

This passion runs through us
Every instant, it is up to
Us to keep the fire
Burning

How and Where Did I Find My Beloved Experience?

I had no clue about love as I know it today. I always thought that what I felt when I was in love was what I needed to feel. What I see clearly now is that the love I felt was usually attached to someone who made me feel good or was who I wanted them to be. The need to be filled up or to be filling someone else with love was the spark that ignited me. Every relationship that I attracted was exciting until issues came up and I was forced to feel the void within me. The experience then became empty or simply shut down.

Every relationship showed me either my neediness for love and attention or my own lack of love. I expected so much and the other person always felt my disappointment. I went to the brink of despair and felt the void in every aspect of my life. Once I felt it fully, however, and took responsibility for it, I realized that it wasn't someone else's love I needed to look for, it was mine.

So I took my time and worked with my formula to release the past that kept me stuck in the density of dark emotions and loneliness. Heavy, suppressed emotions created darkness and a void within me … the disconnection from my own love.

I learned to reach inside myself, through a process of understanding, to find my own love and peace to fill the void and create strong self-worth. This practice enabled me to walk in my world safely, not wait for someone else to do it for me. I began living and walking differently in my life. I felt my own experience and took responsibility. I stopped blaming or judging myself, or anyone else. It was as if fresh air were moving through my body.

When I look back at the different stages of my life, I realize that once I finally felt safe on my own, I was free; I felt no attachments. I didn't know where I was going, I didn't know what the outcome was going to be and I didn't really have a goal. I trusted the plan, trusted that I was going where I had to go and knew my vibration was high. When we work on releasing stuck, dark or dense emotions and we experience the flow of life, we can feel more open than we did before. When we are pulled down by people or experiences that shut us down and our vibration is low, our light can become dim.

Nelson Mandela, who was in jail for 20 years, evolved from the darkness of the prison, beyond his suppressed pain and fear and was able to break out of the prison of his mind. When Nelson Mandela was released, his vibration was extremely high. He became an amazing example of truth and greatness of spirit, a remarkable leader and an inspiration of inner strength.

I had put myself in my own prison of the mind, waiting for someone else to give me back my freedom and spirit. But the strength and life force had to be connected by me and my open heart found my spirit again. I was then able to see the goodness in others and be aware of their fear. I believe we can feel the vibration in another person, their degree of safeness or fear, just as we feel the safeness within. We must take care of our own emotional health and be the silent witness and the example of safe relationship.

The beloved will show his or her face when the time is right and when each of us is ready to see the belovedness in another because we feel it within.

My experience of a relationship in the past had been sparked by romantic love. I believe that romantic love, at the point of ignition, can be overwhelming, overpowering, intoxicating and can feed our neediness. The spark that I felt with Bruce was very gentle. He was so different from any other man I had known in the past. What initially intrigued me when we first met was how comfortable I felt with him. I loved his voice ... the vibration of his energy. His presence was that of a nobleman and he captured my heart. I wasn't quite sure where it was going (which was kind of neat) because I was "in the moment" with it. When I met his daughter Jessica, we instantly felt love and joy together.

After Bruce returned from his trip he called asking me out for dinner and I said, "No! Let's make it lunch," as my old fears began to well up. I didn't want to make the same mistakes I had in the past. I wanted to get to know him slowly.

This experience was new to me – I didn't feel needy with Bruce! My relationships in the past usually triggered self-worth issues in me and their non-committal character would create feelings of abandonment. I often became obsessive and needy for love.

Love cannot be forced

Love cannot be birthed from *fear*

The *fear* can be SHATTERED by Love

Bruce's voice, his words, his peace, his gentleness – there was safety here. I felt safe to explore my heart with him. We went for lunch at Snug Harbor, a beautiful restaurant on the water. It was very busy and when I arrived at the table he handed me a gift – a beautiful orchid in a glass bowl. That was a first!

Bruce and I were totally immersed in our conversation for two and a half hours and I don't even remember what I ate. His stories wove with mine and we were both very present as we got to know each other. By the time we were ready to go, the restaurant was completely empty. When we got to the parking lot, there were only two cars sitting in the huge lot: his and mine, side by side ... It gave me a bit of a jolt. As he opened his car door, Bruce said, "I hope you don't mind, I don't want to scare you away, but in order to get that single orchid I had to buy the whole spray." He reached into the car and handed me the entire spray of orchids. I was blown away! He presented those orchids to me in such a beautiful, humble way, I didn't believe he was doing it just to impress me. I felt very safe wrapped in the fragrance of the orchids as I drove home.

Bruce *had* made a huge impression on me but we took our time getting to know each other. Bruce was a true gentleman and very caring. We dated for three months and he created safe conversation and beautiful times while we slowly and gently opened our hearts.

Every step carefully taken with each other had created a safeness and our truthfulness was the foundation of intimacy. I was different and I felt different in this experience. Bruce was the reflection of the real love in me. I could feel myself reach my higher vibration with him. I knew that he would hold the space and inspire me to be all that I was and I would do the same for him. A constant and comfortable weave of energy would move us through the dark places of our past suppressed emotions and we would hold the space for one another as we moved deeper inside.

When we take care of our own issues and share our past, the beloved relationship takes over and we find a deeper part of ourselves with each other. This continues to re-ignite the relationship. Each layer of the relationship reaches a richer, deeper and safer place. It takes constant dedication to our own deep love in order to ensure a healthy loving experience. We are designed to live in twos, not to fix each other or destroy one another, but to find that sacred space, the container where the beloved lives beyond the pain.

When we make the choice to take care of our own needs and our own darkness, we can then care for the other person, not "fixing" them, but supporting them with our own brave, compassionate heart … from this place within, relationships can survive anything. This safe support can heal the abuse that we've all suffered and we can feel safe to be all that we are with one another.

To feel the rapture of love that is full because it is connected to our self-love, its own source of power … we don't have to take anything from anyone … the beloved existence of one benefits the other.

I have faith in myself and my husband Bruce and pray that we will continue to grow together.

WITHOUT ***Conditions***...... *WITH* ***Another***

One hand touching another is the ultimate prayer.

I never have to look over my shoulder when I'm with Bruce. He's a perfect fit with the person I know myself to be today. I will continue to go to all of the crevices in my heart, living with him and getting to know more of him, as I grow deeper in myself. Bruce is my greatest friend, my passionate lover, and because he takes care of his own darkness, he shines the light for me when I am in mine. I have never experienced a love as deep as the one I know now ... and I know that it is just the beginning. Bruce is my reflection of the Beloved.

WE DON'T KNOW UNTIL WE KNOW

CHAPTER TWO

Falling in Romantic Love

Romantic Love is the initial falling IN love ... you fall (says Dr. Phil, and I agree). However, I believe that you fall **inside yourself** ... the experience connects with "your" feelings of love. The issues that arise from the intensity of romantic love, direct us to **fall in** (inside) ourselves to feel. Romantic love is a wonderful feeling of bliss, passion and attached love that explodes with sexual energy and is woven with romantic illusion. We only see and feel whatever it is we want to experience. This romantic love is a powerful way to get someone's attention, lifting hidden fears and lack of love that have been shoved aside. My experience of being ignited in romantic love created the opportunity to heal my wounded self, by living through the experience of parts of me dying in love, surviving the death of love and realizing my attachment was because I had to have a man to love me. Falling is a sudden shift that creates joyous euphoria or emotional pain. When the shattering occurs, the illusion is blown wide open or one person falls out of the love. That is when you are tested and where you can choose to heal the old wounds of past relationship.

Romantic love is intoxicating and can be a whirlwind in which you can lose yourself as I did. Coming out of a failed marriage, very vulnerable and scared, I was ignited by a man I'll call D.C. I was consumed by him, by his words … I only saw what I wanted to see. It was more love than I had ever felt. I didn't want to do anything else but be with this person. He was my knight in shining armor, taking me away from all of my misery and pain. I was running toward love, away from my past, and I got lost in this relationship. It was total ecstasy and I didn't care about anything else … I needed it. He became my addiction.

When I look back on it, knowing what I know now, D.C. was in the same place as me. He wanted love just as badly as I did. I was his light and I filled him up; he filled me up, too, and we were on an incredible ride fueled by illusion. D.C. wanted it so badly that he controlled everything I did to get love, to get me, and I allowed him to because I wanted it just as much. I wanted this feeling of fullness in me that I believed was him. So I believed everything he said.

Do you believe in love at first sight? Is it physical beauty or loveliness that we see in another, or are we experiencing the energy of the one that is sparking the love inside us – the comfort, the ignition of passion. If we were blind, we would not see the physical beauty of this experience, but we would feel the energy, voice, or breath of the other. Real love is felt and experienced with an inner sight and the inner remembrance of our own love. Take the time to explore what feels good to you so that you can recognize it in another.

Looking Back on Past Relationships with a Healed Heart

So, I threw away everything I believed in and wanted to start over with D.C. I ended my marriage to my children's father, who I blamed, making it easy to leave him. I felt worthy of love, so it was easy for me to say that this was okay. I was "unpresent" in my life, with my children, family and friends. The relationship with D.C. was all consuming and I was under a spell that numbed me. All I wanted was this love! I picked up and left Kitchener as fast as I could to get rid of the pain, running away from my own self. I wanted to start over and create heaven on earth with this man. But things were happening so fast. I would sense signs of discomfort as time went on. I was becoming aware of his control; I could feel the pull.

I SLOWLY STARTED TO LOSE MYSELF
I FELL HARD
INTO THIS **DARK PLACE**

My children experienced upheaval. Lauren was just a baby and Lindsay was about seven. My daughters felt the separation in all aspects of their life. Lindsay was older and she could not feel me very present. I was consumed with the relationship and the guilt.

When I began to see the signs of the unhealthiness of the relationship, I refused to acknowledge them. I was slowly putting myself under his control. Every time I tried to move away from his bond, I would be emotionally flattened. I wanted the love and approval so badly that I kept digging myself into a dark hole. I then began to see his lies and my desperation. I was manipulated and I allowed myself to be the victim. I lost everything in my life that mattered and my health failed. I shut down my love; I was full of anger, resentment and fear. I was caught up on the merry-go-round of life, and in addition, had a business that consumed me and gave the illusion of abundance and freedom. It kept me distracted, but I eventually lost that too.

ONCE THE ROMANTIC LOVE SHATTERED I FELL FROM THE CLOUDS

EVERY DAY THIS RELATIONSHIP
REMINDED ME OF MY VOID

IT WAS EMPTY

I FELT EMPTY

I WAS **DECEIVED** AND **DISHONORED**

I WAS UNHEALTHY IN THE RELATIONSHIP

I SAW THE TRUTH

AROUND ME

I FACED THE TRUTH

IN ME

The relationship with D.C. was unhealthy and I knew it was my neediness that hooked me into it. My lack of self-worth allowed the disrespect – and I didn't respect myself. D.C. eventually ran away from us, leaving me with a huge debt, (thousands of dollars and an abandoned heart and business). I took care of the debt slowly and painfully … it took me years, while I healed my heart and took care of my daughters.

Nine years later, I had an opportunity to take D.C. to court. My husband Bruce is a corporate litigator with a specialty in fraud. I thought this was a sign that I should go after D.C. and make him accountable and prove him wrong. This would have proved me right but I let go of the plan. The courts would have kept me connected to him and the pain. I LET GO!

I see now that this relationship helped me find my way to my own strength and self-worth, my own self-love. The process led me to great healing. I mended myself by creating my own formula to fill the void.

Time provided healing with my children, my family and friends. I started to live authentically and I knew the difference. As I write this story, I know I have let go of D.C. because I no longer blame him or myself.

I spent years letting go of layers of hurt and resentment. The last nine or ten years moved forward as my spirit took my soul for a ride. Life moved through me and sometimes life became stuck in those places that were still hooked into my past and D.C. I now hold the space for my children, so that they can heal and not carry blame, anger and judgment in their bodies. Because of this opening up in me, as I finally let the D.C. experience go, I can say I did love him and I know he loved me. We didn't know how to live without our wounds of desperation, lack of love, control or shut-down. So as I let go of D.C., I let go of the pain, I let go of the money, and I let go of the resentment. The relationship died ten years ago and I have finally let go.

With the help of my formula, I have been able to let go of all relationships that did not honor me or respect me. I now know how to respect myself. I don't want to make anyone else wrong. No one wins unless they take responsibility for their part and expand from the experience to self-love by letting the other person go, without resentment, as the forgiveness opens the heart.

I am not responsible for anyone's love or abundance, whether it be financial abundance or the abundance of love. I am not responsible for being anyone's savior and do not need their love or approval. I have my own.

Connecting to my life force, I ignite this fire, my self-worth in me, knowing who I am and feeling the fullness, the birth of a new self, the birth of more love in my heart. It's opening me, that part that was connected to him, to my father, to any relationship in which I lost my self-worth, my self-love, my self-respect, where I became the good little girl for love. I allow that part of me, the old self, to die. Feeling the ignition and the light, I am in love. I feel my love and now I can be with you authentically, my life, my children, my family, my beloved.

It doesn't matter what the other person does – the behavior or the results – it's about our own experience of what we need to learn for ourselves. I attracted the same experience to show me my void of love. It is our soul, our spirit, that presents the same lesson until we go inside and take responsibility. No one is to blame or to be judged. It is up to me to get the message, learn the lesson and let go of past blame and resentment.

This is the letter that I wrote to D.C. (my second husband), when I finally let go … ten years after the divorce.

Dear D.C.,

I hope that you can take the time to read my letter to you. It is about letting go. What you do with it and how you feel about it will be your own experience.

I know that our marriage ended many years ago, yet my attachment to hurt, resentment, betrayal and disappointment kept the relationship alive in me. I thought if I could hate you and blame you I would feel better. This shut down part of my heart that kept me attached to you and the pain.

It was not until I took responsibility for my part, that my heart could let go and heal. Blaming you kept me stuck and every so often my life would bring me the same issues and I would feel the pain, the holding in my life, all great opportunities to heal my heart. When I realized your lack of love was no different than mine, I could let go bit by bit. Eventually, I came to the revelation and insight that my lack of self-love and self-worth (neediness) attracted our relationship romantically and ended the relationship with betrayal … I betrayed myself.

I didn't speak up or allow my truth to live with you when I really knew what was going on in all aspects of the relationship and I shut down my heart … fear took over. Your desperate need for money was no different than my desperate need for love.

We lost it all together … we lost ourselves in the darkness of fear. We didn't know any other way. I shut down and you left and we both left emotionally. You left me with debt and I am sure your guilt and my resentment kept you away.

DC, I do forgive your soul and I feel my love as I let you go. We had amazing love and incredible pain. I am different because of this experience.

I have created a beautiful life now with a great partner, Bruce. Lindsay and Lauren are fantastic women and I am blessed and grateful they picked me to be their Mom.

I have dropped the court case and trust the money will someday come back to my Dad and me in another way.

DC, if you wish to ever enter Lindsay and Lauren's life, that will be their choice for their own healing of their hearts.

Take gentle care of yourself,

Colleen

Right after the divorce from D.C., I experienced another significant relationship. Falling in love was wonderful. I was more present and I could see and feel the difference in me. I was careful and enjoyed the ignition of my Goddess self. It was an amazing experience to discover the part of me that could love freely and without conditions. Being more present, I could love him with a totally open heart. But the love brought out his darkness and he could not continue in the relationship. He assumed that I could not be there with him in his darkness. This triggered my neediness, as I felt the separation through his distance and his emotional shut-down.

The relationship lingered for a long time, even though he sent me a "Dear Jane" letter to end it. I was very hurt and it came as quite a shock to me because I was in a different place in the relationship. I thought that it was forever. My abandonment issue was connected to my void of love. The relationship didn't move to where I wanted it to go romantically or physically. I couldn't understand why because I felt so much of myself and my love with him. The shattering caused a lot of pain, which created the opening, in time. The experience brought me to my own loneliness and the place in me that felt there was something wrong with me.

"To live is to Love and
to love is to be without fear
of anything.
You do not survive love,
you do not die of love
because death is not dying,
living without love is".

Patrick Ellis
Author of *Dying in Love*

Now, as I look at the relationship, I realize it was sweet pain. The experience showed me that the love was in me and not attached to him. You can be in love and feel the love with another, but if they don't feel it within themselves, it cannot evolve or survive. Two people must feel their own love and their own pain. This is where I finally felt the difference in my connection to love and my beloved within.

The way we feel in the moment when we are abandoned emotionally, physically, or both, is the pathway to our emotional healing. We can use those feelings and the person who created those feelings to move into our wounded self and develop the safeness within. In order to create a safe place for the other person, who can't show up, we must feel the pain and then let go of the attachment to him or her.

This experience connects to the void inside, the place that is empty of love and holds our lack of self-worth. The abandonment wound attracts the experience that is necessary to bring up the void in the relationship. I was in the place of darkness and aloneness that I needed to be in and it was perfect. It was part of my soul's plan for me to go deeper within. I had been in this place of void in relationships many times since I was a little girl, so it was definitely time for me to heal. I took the time to learn about my anger, my fear and my lack of self-love and each person in my life moved me inside to feel these aspects of me – the light and the dark.

Falling in Like

Falling in like is the beginning of taking notice of our differences and our wounds. Falling in love is the first step to creating that intimate relationship with your heart. So when we are ignited, we create the movement inside so that we are conscious of what we are feeling. Fall in like and slowly open your heart to your own love when you are safe. You can then fall in love without giving away your power or taking it from someone. If we take our time, we can see when we start stepping into romantic illusion. The romantic illusion keeps us disconnected from the truth and keeps us unpresent from what we truly need to feel. I thought I was safe until the love was shattered. If one person cannot show up, the truth is, they *aren't* there.

Needy Love

Needy, obsessive behavior means we are waiting for someone else to fill us up. I see it in so many people because I've lived it myself – where we don't feel fulfilled unless we are given to or we feel we have to control others to get the love – and it can be exhausting. This type of relationship is based on fear of not being loved.

When we're attached to this need or a person for love we can become obsessed. It isn't a calm place and it doesn't feel free. On some levels we're suffocating and on others we may feel dutiful. The giver is caught up in giving for love and the needy one feels lack of love, and both are filling the void that craves the love. One person in the relationship loves for both, while the other person isn't showing up, or even calling. When we are needy we cannot be present with our life or family because we are distracted by the desire, hope or need for the missing person's love, attention or approval.

To be codependent on another for love keeps us returning to our void. Survival keeps us attracting the same lesson and our behavior is repeated … this can be death to the self. To survive is to let go and find our own self-connection to our own love and to live fully on our own. Codependency feeds needy love. We can be obsessed with it, feeling good only if we are with the person. This type of loving, however, is unattractive and can push the other person away. When I think about myself in my needy relationships, I see myself as a totally different woman – afraid of not being loved, desperate for someone else to be the one to love me, to give me my breath, to tell me everything was okay. With them in my life I felt special, I felt loved. At the same time, I would feel the separation and the longing, which was my own void. The men I experienced in this way would not show up or call. They would leave me and I would feel abandoned.

IT WOULD HURT

I WOULD FEEL **Disregarded**

I WOULD FEEL **Disrespected**

I felt the experience of my lack of love/worth, the feeling of not being good enough. This type of relationship would bring me to those painful places in my heart that I had closed, places where I needed to feel so I could then learn the process of healing. I had to move inside to connect to my own life force, to take care of my void. Little by little I took back my power, the power that I had given away, and I realized that I didn't need anyone's love – I had my own. I didn't need their approval – I had my own. I wanted love in my life, but I didn't want codependent love anymore. I made the transition from needy love to self-love and this connection was where I healed. The point at which I understood my void, the obsession and the neediness for someone else to love me, was a turning point, creating the process to find my way back inside me, where my own love lived. I could feel the love instead of having to always give to someone in order to get love back.

CHAPTER THREE

The Pocket Guide to Your He♥rt Formula

I have come to understand that this formula, which I have worked with personally for 10 years, completes a process that is absolutely necessary for the daily practice of lightening my heart.

The *Pocket Guide to your He♥rt* formula is made up of three parts:

1. The Inner Relationship – re-connecting with yourself and creating a safe place to feel the truth of your emotions.
2. The Inner Workout – embracing your resentment, fears, anger and unloving thoughts and letting go of the burden of suppressed emotions in a healthy way.
3. Inner Peace – connecting with your own source of inner safe love as you open your compassionate heart, strengthening your

self-worth and self-acceptance. Feeling the Peace in you and with another.

Creating your Future from Peace
AND NOT FROM FEAR

The Inner Relationship

The Inner Relationship is the connection to our emotions, what we feel and how we don't feel.

Meditation – A journey out of your mind's details into your inner relationship.

> *Take a deep breath, close your eyes and allow the rhythm of your breath to take you deep within.*
>
> *Visualize a bridge and see yourself walking toward it. This bridge is your safe place to feel truth; it can appear any way you would like. See nature around you and be conscious of the beauty of the water, woods and the design of your bridge. Feel the safe space within as you walk here, each step and breath bringing you deeper "in you." On the other side of the bridge see the silhouette of a young child…you, when you were 4-8 years old. Remember her/him as you walk closer…feel your heart welcome your younger self…create a safe place for him/her.*
>
> *Hold her/him in the way you yearn to be held.*

Feel how much he/she misses you…it has been a long time.

Can you love him/her?

Talk to your child…he/she is the symbol of your emotions…

Feel…open to what your heart needs to experience and speak from this place.

If you feel loneliness…feel it…allow yourself to feel it…

If you feel fear…allow the fear to come…

If there is hurt or disappointment…speak about these emotions while you talk to him or her.

Create the connection and allow the love to expand your heart.

Talk to him/her and tell this child how safe this relationship will be.

You will not abandon him/her any longer.

No one has to take care of him/her from now on…you will be the parent…you will protect her/him…feel this connection everyday.

You will show this child how to love (this child is a symbol of your emotions).

This safe inner connection opens the pathway to the inner workout.

The Inner Workout

The Inner Workout creates the experience of feeling and speaking about truth and uncomfortable emotions as we use the people in our lives who have triggered experiences or emotions that took us out of peace or who have hurt us.

> *Bring someone onto the imaginary bridge with whom you need to speak the truth. Feel them as if they were in front of you. Feel, cry, react, project, confront until you empty yourself of dense emotions. Feel it in your body. Look into their eyes and feel the energy of this experience. See an emotional cord connected to this person and when you feel the depth of the heavy emotions, count to three and cut the cord. One, two, three...cut it yourself. Re-connect with your life force...take back your power. Move into your heart and look into the eyes of this person. You've just taken responsibility for your part. Forgive him/her and forgive yourself. Open your heart and feel the compassion. You don't need their approval, you don't need their love... you have it yourself...it is in you. Let them go and hold your little girl or little boy. Feel the love and the safeness in you as you re-connect, as you feel your open heart, feel your own life force. Standing in front of this person on the bridge, feel the space within. Inspire them as you stand before them with an open heart.*

Create the place in you of peace

For the beloved to recognize

The beloved in you.

The Inner Workout is a daily practice to keep you emotionally fit by clearing the heaviness of suppressed emotions and disconnecting from the past relationships in your life. Use your family, take each one of them onto the bridge – your mother, father, sisters, brothers, your intimate circle. Whether you see them or not, whether they've passed on or not, doesn't matter. Take them onto the bridge and go through the same Inner Workout exercise to see what suppressed resentment, hurt and pain may be in your body. Whether it's disappointment, shame, guilt, blame, judgment, anger or lack of self-love – FEEL – take the time with the process to clear these things out of your body so that you don't have to attract discomfort into your life. You can then live more centered and connected to your own peace.

Take each significant relationship, a boyfriend or girlfriend, that you've had in your life and do the same thing – confront them on the bridge. There might be some past disappointment, anger, lack of self-worth, loneliness, fear or the void that you felt with them. Recognize that each of these people from your past that you bring onto the bridge has revealed a part of yourself to you over and over again. This is the process of moving into your emotions, by feeling their energy, remembering the relationship, disconnecting from it by cutting the cord to them and connecting to your own life force. Feel the fire within your root (see page 108) and allow this energy to come up through your body and your heart so that you can move into compassion, as you let go of them and let go of the experience living in you.

> *Each of these relationships that we still carry in our life, in our body, in our heart, is there because we are still attached to the blame or anger, resentment or hurt. We need to go through this process to let go so that they are no longer alive in us. The memories of these relationships can close our hearts and may be the reminder of our void or our own pain. This exercise is very important to find our way to our open space where the beloved experience lives.*

If we were emotionally or physically abused, rejected or betrayed, we need to bring the person onto the bridge to do the Inner Workout and release the emotions in our body.

I believe that if we have the memories and the hurt of rejection in our bodies, we will continue to attract it.

I believe that we attract these unloving experiences to make us feel the void within and to feel the place where we do not love ourselves. Once we go through these levels of healing and let go, we can then feel stronger in our self-worth, having more space within to feel more love.

The Inner Workout is the pathway to Inner Peace.

Inner Peace

Inner Peace is the result of going through the pathways of the Inner Relationship and the Inner Workout. This exercise routine can develop your inner safeness and confidence to create the experience of releasing and re-connecting with your own self and the divine power within.

Once you have cut the dense emotional cord, move your awareness back to your root area where your life force can be re-connected – the memory of the energy of passion and purpose that lives in you. Feel this fire and breathe into your fullness ... feel your open heart and experience the forgiveness and self acknowledgement ... enjoy this peace ... you are worthy of love ... it is alive in you. Rest in this place that waits to be embraced and allow this moment of unconditional love to open the pathway of the beloved.

When we are connected to the knowledge of who we are and to our own belief system, we are then open to see more. No one can ever destroy this connection to our self. If we choose, while in our pain or in our lack of self-worth, to allow someone to take away our power, in the next breath, we can take it back.

The Pocket Guide to your He♥rt formula can be your daily practice to help you stay connected.

When I look in my journal and read about my relationships since I was a young girl, I see that the issues I was dealing with were all the same, creating the same dance. Every experience and relationship took me to different realities and truths that I needed to face and aspects of me I needed to own. I feel differently about myself now and my shifted perception has opened me to more love. Every relationship took me to truth or untruth. Each experience brought me inside to feel and if I was uncomfortable, I used my formula to take care of myself and the emotions that weighed so heavily.

If you are in a relationship that pulls you down, use the experience and the person to find your way to your own health and open heart. Be a user. Take the uncomfortable present that hooks onto your painful past and use the people in your life to feel, clear and let go. Use your relationships to heal ... take a walk on the bridge.

THE BELOVED

> **The Beloved** is neither a person nor a place. It is an experience of deeper and deeper levels of being, and eventually of Beingness itself – **the boundarylessness of your own great nature expressed in its rapture and absolute vastness by the word "love."** Author Unknown

Find your complete comfort of the beloved within. When struggle arises with another you can find your way past the fear to your open heart. Your daily process can soften the threshold with your beloved partner.

Case Study: ***Maria and John***
Issues: Neediness, Betrayal and Infidelity

Maria is a client who was very needy for love. Maria is a beautiful woman and her abandonment issues led her to search for truth about herself. She lost her father when she was a year old so she never really knew what it was like to have a father. She had a great desire and need for the love of a man. Her mother never remarried and there were no other men in the picture. Maria went searching for the attention and love. She used her sexual energy and her vulnerability to attract men. She was so needy for love that she was eventually abused and abandoned emotionally by the relationships. The men she attracted filled her initially, wooing her and making promises. But they would eventually leave her emotionally, shut down or not be available.

Women who have this vulnerability, like Maria, have been abused emotionally or sexually, creating "unsafeness" with men: lack of trust and disappointment. The person needy for love often attracts relationships that bring up abandonment issues, their void of love, lack of self-respect, and their lack of self-worth. Maria attracted unavailable men, men who would either drink, abuse her physically or sexually, or men who would be unavailable emotionally. This pattern continued to recapture the past that stemmed from the void she experienced with her father, never knowing what it was like to have a gentle, loving, respectful, honoring relationship with a man. Maria didn't have the experience of safe, real love; she didn't know it within or know how to live it.

Maria's fear and unsafeness led her to judge herself and others, adding to the addiction of needy love. Maria would do anything, at any cost, to have this love, even if it was with someone like John, who was unavailable and married. The pain and the loneliness in this relationship shut her heart down when she wasn't with him and she was distracted from aspects of her life. Her struggle with guilt and resentment kept her closed to hearing truth or her inner voice. Maria would let go of John, and his promises would pull her into feeling needy again.

Maria used the Inner Workout to take John to the bridge many times a week and used this unhealthy relationship to strengthen her self-worth and move into her heart of love. She would invite John onto her bridge as she visualized the relationship, to feel the pain, the guilt and the unworthiness. She would talk to John in this place inside, feeling the loneliness and the pain of the relationship. She spoke to him as if he were right there, moving these tough emotions that she had been carrying in her body since she was a little girl. Maria slowly took back her power and said, " No, I can't be there." She let go on many levels, saying, "No! It's not enough." She had to deal with her guilt of betrayal because John was married. Maria brought his wife onto the bridge and faced her guilt, anger and shame.

This pattern often happens with women and men who leave their unhappy marriages. They are needy for love, so they have an affair, thus moving further away from any hope of healing their own issues of abandonment, disappointment and lack of self-love because they blame their partner. The husband may go to the arms of another woman, both of them doing everything they can to get the needy love. This distraction can become the addiction to love outside ourselves. It's where we feel good when someone else is giving us the opportunity to feel love. The ignition is what we yearn for, until we realize who we are hurting, including ourselves.

We have to take responsibility for why our relationship is not working and what we haven't done for ourselves. This is the place where people often forget about the other person because they are in a state of blame and judgment, not taking responsibility for their part. I believe relationships are fifty/fifty and it is up to us to take responsibility for our part and take care of our suppressed anger, suppressed fears, past pains and resentments.

Your partner may have disregarded or disrespected you, causing you to shut down. You may have shoved these feelings aside because you were too afraid to speak up about it and have a voice in the relationship. The projection of uncomfortable anger can make you feel not good enough and not connected to your own high vibration or open heart. Stand up in this relationship and say, "I can't be here until you stop disrespecting me." Respect yourself and stand up for yourself, instead of being afraid of losing the love or approval.

We often choose to blame the other person for our pain. We leave the relationship emotionally and then eventually physically. If we could talk with the partner and say, this is why I can't be with you, we would say, "If you cannot take care of your own anger, if you cannot open up and communicate with me, if you cannot share your life with me, have intimacy, if it's not safe to do that, then it's time for me to move on."

Ask for help or counseling together, or find a practice or tool that can help you move into an honoring, respectful place together. Talk as friends instead of dumping, blaming, projecting or demeaning the other person. Eventually the person who is constantly being criticized will leave or shut down. A relationship that is needy for love, void of self-worth or unhealthy in communication will not grow ... It will die.

Find your own self-love and stand up and say, "I'm done. I've talked enough about it and I've shared with you how I feel." Instead of shutting down and leaving the relationship by being unfaithful, create the opportunity for truth and empower one another. BEFORE you walk into the arms of another person, face the music. You had a part in creating this situation. You can only do your best and it's okay if that's not perfect. Accept where you've been in relationship and learn from it.

Every relationship that is created from neediness can become an addiction and can attract infidelity and betrayal on both sides. Secrecy and untruths create unhealthy barriers between two people. It is our choice to be private, but secrets usually come to the surface. If we have anything to hide, this information cuts off the circulation of love and creates a place between two people that can sit there like a time bomb. You never know when someone will slip. We're all human and we all make mistakes.

Maria's experience with John brought up feelings from all the relationships she'd had in the past, revealing all aspects of herself. She was able to release the pain through the Inner Workout, by going to the bridge and creating a safe place to speak the truth and re-connect with her own self-love each time, filling the void and empowering herself. She took back her power and honored and respected herself little by little. She forgave herself and John, letting him go. This process can create a healing ground for neediness and a broken heart.

I now realize that when my partner was unfaithful, the experience allowed me the time to heal my self-worth and my anger. My desperate, low vibration attracted people and experiences that caused me to be abandoned, rejected, and disappointed. The more I could fill my own need for love, create independence, self-respect and connect to my own wounded heart, the more I created a new awareness of self-love. Each relationship was a blessing that changed my perception and redirected my life.

Case study: ***Rosie and Sam***
Issues: Abandonment, Neediness & Insecurity

Rosie is an amazing, very put-together woman but every time she went to a party, she felt her husband eyeing other women. This made her so jealous she shut down and became angry.

Rosie was stifled in the relationship, afraid of Sam's anger and fearful she would lose him. She was not truthful with Sam. She would hide things from him, especially when they concerned money. Rosie was very needy and realized how inauthentic she was with Sam and her life.

Rosie arrived at a weekend retreat very eager and excited. On the first evening as it got dark, people started introducing themselves and sharing their feelings.

Suddenly Rosie felt like running, and she did. She left, she cried, she just couldn't be there ... Rosie was afraid and she realized that she had never been away from her husband, never experienced her own independence, because she was a prisoner in the relationship.

Rosie stayed and worked through all of her hard emotions and found her way back to her own safeness. Her process of self-discovery led her to her abandonment issues and her neediness for love. Rosie's fear of being alone created the experience of being totally alone in her relationship. As she did her Inner Workout and released her past, Rosie stopped blaming Sam for being the keeper of the key to the prison and she began to be more truthful and open. Rosie felt her connection to her self-worth and self-love and when she returned home there was a shift. Sam felt her openness and they fell in love again. Rosie was a lot more open, making Sam feel safe so he didn't shut down. The flirting stopped and her relationship with Sam was re-ignited. Rosie's own shift in disposition made her more attractive and appealing and Sam wanted to spend more time with her. They felt safe with each other. The relationship blossomed into a true beloved relationship with more fun, passion and love.

Background – Rosie's relationship with her mother was shut down and she felt emotionally abandoned and unloved. Her father left and abandoned both of them. Rosie didn't have a relationship with her father and this created feelings of insecurity with men who reflected her void and abandonment issues. Rosie never felt good enough and she became a people pleaser and a caretaker. Eventually, in the relationship with Sam, she felt her disappointment, shutting down from him, not just herself. Sam then stopped filling Rosie up and started feeling needy for attention outside of the relationship, so he flirted. He felt her anger, so he became controlling. His suppressed anger shut him down and Rosie felt abandoned again.

This made her want more things to make her comfortable so Rosie would lie to him when she went shopping and spent more money. She told him part truths, but always cushioned them. Rosie became inauthentic and Sam felt unsafe, as more and more, she felt his disappointment and he felt hers.

The more intimate Rosie became with herself, the more she could open the door to create a safe place without judgment or attachment. Sam could feel safe and open to that part in himself, without resentment or feelings of guilt, so he slowly relaxed.

The safe place in the relationship can be the harbor for healing. If one person is holding the space and taking care of herself or himself, the other person does not have to feel "triggered." Instead, they can inspire one another. Rosie and Sam took responsibility for their suppressed emotions and they stopped blaming each other and stopped shutting down. If one person shifts within and finds their self-love/worth, they can act as the reflection of the relationship ... but he or she might have to leave to find the deep beloved experience with another. It takes two to waltz.

Different Expressions of Needy Relationships

There are different expressions of neediness ... An obsession with love can also be experienced as losing yourself and your desires as you settle for the crumbs that are offered in the relationship. Since childhood we have received, settled and waited for the love that was offered or shown to us because that's all we knew. Not sure of what unconditional love was, I waited for love in the guise of a smile or kind loving word. I didn't feel safe at times.

- The desperate one who needs someone else for their own happiness can be very unappealing.
- Not having a voice because you choose not to speak your truth for fear of losing the love is another sign of a needy heart.
- Fear is holding you back from living free. We think it's another person controlling or holding us back, but it's our own self-doubt that holds us back from speaking our truth.

In the beginning when we are inexperienced with relationship, one person may shut down initially and then the other person does too. It can be uncomfortable when the other person is closed and we plug into them and take it personally. One of us may try to open the other or try to fix them. It might work for a moment, but not long term because the issues are still there. The person who is bringing the love, trying to create the happy safe place and trying to initiate or ignite the love, will get tired of always trying to open that door. In this place of emotional pain we have an opportunity to be with that pain and feel what is going on inside us.

CHAPTER FOUR

Soul Mates

I believe that we can have many soul mates in our life, each relationship becoming a part of our soul's evolution. Soul mates bring us to different levels of ourselves until we reach the beloved experience within, the ultimate partnership. Soul mates can be stepping-stones to the beloved experience. I have met couples who have stayed together through the struggle and have evolved into the beloved experience.

When people think of a soul mate, they think of soul meaning one, the only one. A soul mate is a mate for your soul, your partner – at this time – to take you to the next level. It really doesn't matter whether it is a level of pure love or darkness, it's what you have attracted and it is where you are now. You may attract a soul mate with whom you have no struggles, no apparent issues and everything seems happy. Suddenly, out of the blue, your partner leaves you and you had no clue that he or she was unhappy. This blow hurts deeply and the shock leaves you confused. This wake-up call should take you inside your heart to look at yourself and ask why you didn't notice the signs. No one leaves a comfortable, loving relationship. It takes two to make or break a relationship.

People say I have found my soul mate ... THE END ... that's it. I don't think we can ever say that finding our soul mate is the end of the journey. If two people are in relationship, with their souls continuing to evolve and grow, they will remain in that experience until something shifts or shatters the relationship. If one person stops growing emotionally in the relationship, it is up to the other to make the choice to find another place to heal and to find their higher vibration. It's our choice!

The soul mate relationship is a significant relationship that creates an opportunity for powerful emotional work.

I believe that two willing people, ignited in their own love can experience the dance of past pain and the dance of present joy together.

The Dance

TO SHOW UP TO DANCE
TOGETHER
IS THE GREATEST EXPERIENCE

One of us may stop dancing for a short time –
To take a breath or two ...
Patiently waiting
For the song of love
to ignite the moment
with safe arms and
beating hearts.
THIS PASSION RUNS THROUGH US...
EVERY INSTANT...
IT IS UP TO US...
TO KEEP THE FIRE BURNING

Garth Brooks' song The Dance *reminds me that when we are enjoying a loving relationship we may not be sure how long it will last. He says, "I could have missed the pain but I would have missed the dance." I believe the dance of relationship can show us love and pain. We might not know what we had until we lose it.*

Garth also sings that with her he felt like a King. Unfortunately the King falls. Feeling his pain, he wonders whether he would have done something different if he knew then what he appreciates now.

He confirms that his life is better because he chose to experience the dance of relationship, even though the ending was painful.

Don't let the fear of failure cause you to miss The Dance. *Have the courage to show up, step onto the dance floor and experience the thrill of dancing.*

The pain we feel in relationships can keep us locked in past experiences, keeping us stuck by blaming or judging another. When this happens we abandon ourselves and we shut down our own heart. We should use this experience to feel our past suppressed emotions and re-connect with who we are. Connect to this dark place inside instead of plugging into the other person.

The dance of relationship takes us inside to heal, moving us forward, otherwise we'll end up creating the same experience over and over until we do it differently. It just takes one to shift the dance between two.

Each past relationship still lived in me because I had not forgiven, or could not let go of the memories of the pain. This attachment shut down my heart as I held onto anger, resentment or hurt ... the thought of them would close my heart.

Once I learned to forgive and let go, I had more space for love. The love I had with this man was my own love ... not his. I could then FEEL more of my heart and remember the joy of the relationship. I took the time to heal my wounded heart and saw how my past relationships created the dance of love and the dance of pain. The love gave me strength to feel my pain. It was mine to feel fully and each man created an opportunity for the healing of my soul.

This book explores aspects of ourselves that we create in relationship that cause separation from the beloved within. Once we understand and get to know ourselves more fully, we can move away from old patterns that keep us disconnected from our own love within. Try to look at each relationship as a soul mate connection ... each one essential for the evolution of your soul.

CHAPTER FIVE

Self-Discovery in Relationships

13 Relationship Types

What type of relationship do you want?

What type of relationship do you recognize?

1. The Unavailable Relationship

In an *unavailable* relationship, your partner doesn't show up, doesn't call and is never there, unless he or she wants something or it suits their agenda. In this relationship you may feel the disappointment of always waiting for the other person to appear, and no matter how many times you talk to them about not showing up their behavior doesn't change. They aren't *available* for themselves so they create this experience within and for their partner.

Recognize that you may be *unavailable* to yourself. Are you taking the time to be with you? Are you feeling your open heart? Can you respect yourself and say, "This isn't good enough?" Are you staying in the relationship but feeling like you're talking to a wall, repeating the same communication over and over? The void you feel in this experience is the memory of the relationship you may have had with your mother/father or both, because they were busy and did not choose to love.

Be *available* to yourself and show up for you. Don't settle for crumbs. Say, "This is not what I want!! It's not what my soul yearns for. How will I grow personally if I am stuck?" Use this relationship to stand up for what you deserve and allow your self-worth to grow. Empower yourself by saying, "This is not good enough." Inspire the other person by showing them how to do it differently.

You may be creating a busy life for yourself because you don't want to feel your void, the emptiness or the density of suppressed past hurt.

Be available to yourself! We can become so disconnected from our own source of love that we surrender our power, creating a very uncomfortable experience. In that way, we give others power over us to control how we feel.

IT IS NOT THEIR LOVE
IT IS OUR LOVE THAT WE FEEL.
EACH RELATIONSHIP IS THE OPPORTUNITY
TO LOVE MORE
OR LOVE LESS

If you find you are waiting for someone to show up or call, take this time and connect to what it brings up for you. Be the one to show up for yourself and this will attract the one who knows how to show up for you. If you wait for someone to give you the attention or love, you may be disappointed.

2. The Lonely Relationship

We can feel lonely even when we are in a relationship. Take, for example, the husband who is a workaholic in his career and fills up his life with work. The wife is unpresent in the relationship when her husband comes home because she is giving all of her attention to the children. She may be tired or busy and there is no space for the husband or time for intimacy with him. They both feel lonely and disconnected; they feel their void of love in the relationship and in themselves.

Alone can be beautiful! When we are in relationships we need time to be alone, time with ourselves. If this becomes all the time, however, then we're not participating with each other. There is a difference between feeling lonely and being alone. If you feel lonely in the relationship, then consider how you're not attracting what your soul needs to feel alive. The choices you might make if you depend on someone else to fill your loneliness could continue to attract a lonely life if you are only connected to that part in you that is needy for love, afraid of being alone or lonely.

3. Separate Bedrooms... Separate Lives

Some couples have separated so much within the relationship that they have absolutely no desire to be together; they don't even like each other. They haven't had a chance to move beyond the issues that trigger each other, leaving the relationship unfulfilling. I've had some clients who lived that way until they woke up and said, "I do want more. I do want to have a fulfilling relationship." In a separated relationship, without intimacy, they may look outside for love, living inauthentically with their partner.

4. The Shut-Down Relationship

One or both are shut down, reflecting a closed heart because neither wants to project the pain. They think that not saying anything and shutting down their heart is going to protect the other person and protect themselves. This creates a wall around the heart and a barrier in the relationship. One of the partners needs to find their way to their open heart and inspire the other. If the other person doesn't take responsibility to let go of their anger or resentment, the closed heart will eventually shut down the relationship.

Some men have learned the shut-down, perhaps from their father or mother, or both parents – and this was their first experience of relationship. A woman may recognize that her partner is shut down because she witnessed her mother or father live it.

We cannot open the other person, we can only open ourselves. Our inspiration and loving open heart can be the example.

5. The Angry Relationship

Projecting or acting out anger is toxic. Some people suppress their anger all day long, wearing an inauthentic mask, and then come home to project anger on their family. Some people say, "My partner is always angry" yet their behavior is pleasant. They suppress their anger.

We all have anger. How do we take care of it? Do we suppress it or project it? Either way is inappropriate. An angry relationship could look like this: one person projects their anger, the other person shuts down and shoves aside their anger, feeling the resentment, until one day the one who is suppressed explodes because they can't contain it any longer. Do we give our anger to our children or partners?

We need to take care of our anger in a healthy way. Our children learn this explosive anger dance from their experience growing up. Some people think that anger is okay to project, but it is NOT! Suppressed anger is not healthy either. It will eventually hurt us or someone else, causing illness and separation. Anger is unattractive and suppressed resentment keeps us inauthentic. Both are the source of unhealthy relationships and unhealthy bodies.

Let go of anger and resentment and re-connect with your own self-love and self-worth.

6. Needy

Someone who is feeling empty or lonely may look for someone or something to fill the void of love. This person searches for love outside themselves. Needy love feeds inauthentic behavior and is unattractive. The man or woman who wants love so badly will do anything for it. When feeling needy this person may behave like a little boy or a little girl, demanding attention or fulfilling someone else's needs so that they are loved. Our void of love within can create a desperate experience needy of love.

7. The Unfaithful Relationship

We may attract an unfaithful experience with untruth and denial. We might not want to believe our gut feelings. The dance of guilt and resentment will create "unsafeness" in the relationship. If you've attracted this experience, you are probably not comfortable with truthful communication. Relationships woven with lies, hidden agendas or infidelity lack trust. The one who lives this way has created a pattern of self-hatred and guilt. The one who is experiencing this from their partner feels unsafe and is living with resentment and fear. Both behaviors are reflections of lack of self-love: the one who hurts and the one who feels hurt. Why do we disrespect another and why do we disrespect ourselves? The Inner Workout can strengthen your self-worth to say, "No! This is not good enough."

8. The Unsafe, Abusive Relationship

This type of experience is woven with judgment and criticism and plays a big part in low self-esteem. Can we love ourselves enough to say no to any type of abuse or unsafe relationships? Emotional, sexual or physical abuse is not appropriate. Any relationship where you feel uneasy is telling you to recognize that you are in an unsafe place. Listen to your body, how you feel and how comfortable you are. Take care of yourself. I have had many clients who were abused as children, but they didn't have the awareness or strength to say no. As adults, they have attracted abuse and this practice of visualizing a bridge, finding their safe place and confronting their abuser to express the fear and pain gives them an opportunity to create the courage within to say no in their present relationship.

Addictive relationships and addictive personalities will attract each other. If we are addicted to love because of our neediness, we may attract an addictive personality who drinks too much, does drugs or betrays us in some way, mirroring our void and our addiction to love. Our addictive personality may need a quick fix and no one can fix us. We must say NO and take care of ourselves. Create the safe, healthy environment inside and out. If someone goes beyond the safe boundaries, STAND UP AND SAY NO!!!

Take responsibility and stop the abuse.

9. The Waiting Experience

This is the experience of waiting for the other person to change. I'll be happy when he/she does this or that, or, I'll be happy when he/she changes, believing he/she is the one who needs to be fixed. We can't change anyone; we can only change ourselves. Stop, look and listen. What are you waiting for? If someone doesn't show up for themselves or you, move on, move inside and show up for yourself. Stop whining about them and take care of yourself.

10. Abandonment Relationship

We feel our void in this relationship type. It is the relationship that doesn't show up, disappears unexpectedly or is not there emotionally or physically. The abandonment could be death, it could be separation, loss of some sort or just the experience of feeling the void of love with another. This person is the reminder of our own void, so we need to use him/her and take them onto the bridge to feel the pain and the hurt. As children, we were all abandoned physically or emotionally on some level. Let go of attachments to others for love and connect with your own source within. Fill your own void of love and use these abandoned relationships to feel the pain. Don't abandon yourself.

11. The Reward/ Punishment Relationship

This type of relationship is very unsafe because we don't know when we will be punished or rewarded. When we are rewarded, we believe that we are loved and when we are punished we feel the lack of love. We learned this as a child, becoming the good little boy/girl for love. This type of experience makes us feel like the bad girl or boy. This type of relationship is unattractive and an unhealthy way to love, creating tension and unsafeness.

12. The Second Marriage

We will attract the same issues in the next relationship until we have healed them in ourselves. If we have not healed our past issues, we will find ourselves in the same relationship of struggle. We attract what we are and what we need to heal. If we take the time in the relationship to heal ourselves instead of blaming the other person or shutting down, the next relationship has a chance to dance differently, creating commitment and the Beloved Experience.

13. The Beloved Relationship - Peaceful and Loving

The Beloved is in you and when you are living with your own peace, with the connection to self-love and self-worth, you can attract your reflection. The *Pocket*

Guide to your He♥rt formula can create inner peace with each relationship type. When you feel empty, needy for love, disappointed or angry, re-connect within. Use the relationship to feel the inner emotions that stop you from feeling your open heart. The formula takes us to the bridge where truth and untruth can be felt.

The Inner Workout creates a personal experience to confront and let go of past hurts and resentments that shut down communication. Connect with your compassionate heart as you forgive and allow your source of love and peace to set you free. Make healthier choices for healthy relationships.

What do you want your reflections to look like?

Take some time and write about your past and present relationships. Recognize any of these 13 experiences within the relationships and feel, let go and forgive. Find your way to the beloved within.

I chose relationships to find my beloved experience

Every relationship is a reminder of our own love or the love that we've shut down in our hearts. By opening ourselves up to that relationship, and letting go, we can also open up to more love in our heart. Each partner can be a reminder of the love or a reminder of the lack of love, and each expression is important for our personal growth.

I lived all 13 relationship types with three significant men in my life. Each experience opened up a part of me because I went to the past pain and the love. I now see each of them as perfect gifts for my soul's evolution. When I let go of blame, I felt more love and peace. My Spirit is living a higher vibration because of them. I attracted my beloved Bruce because of my experiences with all of my past relationships.

CHAPTER SIX

Victim, Bully, Needy, Peaceful

A relationship of love and pain will show us different aspects of ourselves. Once we face personal issues that are acted out in behaviors and misbehaviors, we can unhook from the people who trigger us. When we see it in another we must recognize that it is in us as well.

A **Victim** is one who is shut down and may never feel that he or she is good enough. The energy is of “poor me, I’m hard done by.” Victim shut-down can also control someone in a relationship ... controlling for attention and playing the blame game. *The victim is unattractive.*

The **Bully** is the one that projects anger, controls, or manipulates the relationship showing disappointment in another person. This personality creates an unsafe environment, forcing people to walk on eggshells and become inauthentic. The bully or petty tyrant also creates fear within the relationship and always needs to be right. The words *I'm sorry* are difficult to express. *A bully type is NOT attractive.*

The **Needy** person will do anything for love, lose themselves in the relationship, and do everything to make the other person happy or comfortable. A caretaker personality mothers the other person for love. The needy one wants love so badly they often control to get love. For the needy person there is never enough attention. No one can make them happy. *The needy personality can be obsessive or addictive and is extremely unattractive!*

We can all attract or become **Victim, Bully**, or **Needy** in our relationships. Each is fueled by the fear of not being loved and each is controlling.

The **Peaceful** person provides the most attractive relationship experience. Peace is in each of us and can be the reflection between two people as they learn to connect with their inner peace.

Victim, Bully, Needy = UNATTRACTIVE
Peaceful = ATTRACTIVE

CHAPTER SEVEN

Self-Worth

Our journey to self is the process of learning to let go of the control and the resentments that shut us down. Anger is toxic and separates us from the connection to self-love.

Self-love creates peace

Self-love + Peace = SELF-WORTH

What uncomfortable places does relationship take you?

Self-worth / Self-doubt issues

– Disregarded

– Betrayal

– Emptiness and aloneness

– Control

– Fear

– Anger

– Lack of self-love (our void)

Take Responsibility

The places that feel good and content are in me. The issues that shut me down or the parts in another that I don't like are in me. Can I connect with all these parts in me?

BE THE LOVE

Take responsibility for everything and everyone that you have attracted into your life. Try to stop blaming others for your pain. Let go of judging others or yourself and observe without attachment. Forgive the person who stops you from loving fully and find the way to your open heart.

In self-discovery we have to ask, "What truly makes me happy?" It's important to know what our desires are for a relationship. Make a list of all the things you want and hope for in your relationship and then BE them.

Hope

Hope has no attachments and can be our future. Hope is embraced with self-worth, leading us to each relationship.

If I only knew then what I know now! How easy it would have been! When we fully embrace our past experiences, we can move into the present and be free to look back on our past and see why we were the way we were – why we reacted and how we misbehaved.

This awareness brings us wisdom and the confidence to stay connected to our own source of love and inner peace. Hope weaves our present into our future.

Control

Don't *fix*

Don't *control*

Be in truth

Don't *shut down*

Don't *blame*

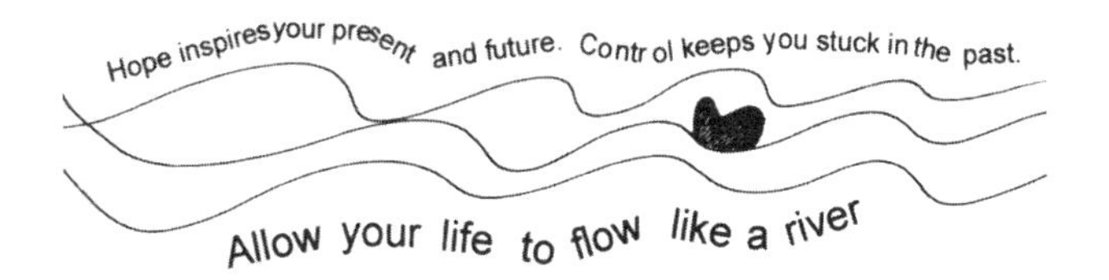

Try not to control your life or anyone else's. Control keeps us from opportunity and new experiences. Control will stop the flow of ease between two people. Letting go of control allows the space for each person to take care of themselves and honor and respect themselves and their partner. Let go of control. Feel free to speak the truth without blame or judgment. Each of us has our own past to be felt in the present. By feeling the emotions that life brings, we can eventually release them.

Don't plug into one another, plug into your own emotional self and connect with your own love. Feel your own love within the relationship – this ignition can remind your partner of the love if they forget, holding the space for them to be where they need to be. Let go of control and allow life to move through you, flowing like a river, and relax as you live present.

Bridge the past and the present. If we are willing to let go of our past over and over again, we will experience growth and change. Then we can evolve out of the space we are in and move forward. We may feel like we are going backwards for a time but beyond the fire of uncomfortable emotions comes more space with more love and peace. We may be asleep, living in illusion and numbed out, not very satisfied with life and relationships. When we wake up to the truth of our own unhappiness we are able to move forward without our past anger and resentments. From this level of truth, our connection to the innocent child within creates a safeness to continue to see our own reflection and to get to know who we truly are.

Everyone and each experience that triggers our fears and pain in the present are connected to our past. Use the present to heal your past.

CHAPTER EIGHT

Breathe on Your Own

It took me 49 years to come to the realization that I MADE the choice to breathe on my own. I'm a triplet and when I was born I stopped breathing. The doctors put the three of us into one incubator, with me in the middle between my sisters Frannie and Philomene. I was told all my life that their kicking kept me alive and I believed that I needed my sisters, my family, my children, my friends, my vision or my work to keep me breathing. My sister Frannie reminded me that **I made the choice to breathe** and that I had always done it on my own. It was a great revelation to me because I was so conditioned and programmed to believe that I couldn't breathe on my own. I had always attracted relationships where I felt I needed the other person so I could breathe fully, or they had to believe in my vision of life to give me my breath. This fed me and filled me up. I also believed that each person I was in relationship with needed me to help them breathe.

I can breathe for myself and I can let everyone else breathe on their own.

Our breath connects us to everything we are.

Freedom of Your Heart

The mind and ego are powerful tools as we control, fix or manipulate life. As I observe the passage of experiences in another, I quickly and compassionately remember my process of getting from A to BE. Today I can be the witness and know deep within there is another way ... one that flows through me instead of attaching to past issues.

When a past experience is relived, can I not judge the person or experience and know that I am okay? In that moment, can I remember that they don't feel good about themselves? They may be expressing themselves the only way they know how.

Instead of figuring it out, I like to *feel it out*. Each experience in our life takes us inside to feel.

Each experience and every person that comes into my life can show me a part of myself that I love or a part of me I don't. To take the time to get to know people without judgment means staying in my heart to experience myself through them.

Someone may bring us to our own discomfort of past pain or even emptiness.

We will experience the same feelings until we own them and take care of them. Going inside to feel uncomfortableness may not be your first choice. But try it. You might see the shift in your life if you do. This change of perception can attract a healthier, happier life. See your experiences as an opportunity to feel, instead of a challenge to fix.

Listen

Take time to listen! Listen to others; create the safe place to get to know yourself deeply by being a good listener. The busy performer or convincer doesn't take time to connect to himself or another. Create the space in your life to feel you and to feel that part in you that your outside world is reflecting. Feel the fear and the love in each experience. Listen to what the silence or noise is telling you.

Confidence/Self-Worth

Go within
Feel the freedom of your heart
without
attachment or judgment.

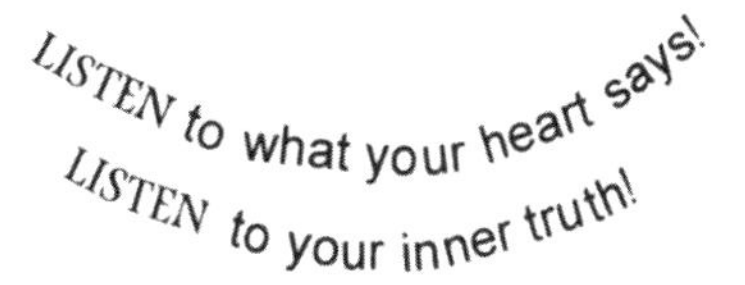

What we feel on the inside affects how we feel with the outside.

Confidence is a state of being that has developed with our personality. Our identity and persona are the connection to our life experiences. If we have to walk through a door of opportunity we can move with confidence to achieve something.

If we feel good about ourselves, our connection to self-worth embraces the opportunity with comfort, like a healthy relationship. Confidence can definitely take action as the mind attaches to the outcome. Self-worth never denies self-love and in the moment of an uncomfortable experience, self-worth can be tested and sometimes forgotten. Our egos can perceive the worst about ourselves and can stop us from feeling the connection of self-love and self-worth.

I look at personal past experiences and can remember how I felt about myself as I felt judgment from another – or assumed their judgment. An experience may cause another person to shut down or become embarrassed. Our feelings and our perceptions belong to us, not to others … and we do sometimes assume the worst.

Confidence
combined with self-worth
creates a very attractive persona.

Your Presence

Living in the present moment creates a presence of love and peace in us. This connection to the *now* feels peaceful and centered because the memories of our past have woven with the essence of who we are now and with the knowingness of a future designed uniquely for us.

We can become this presence by using the *Pocket Guide to your He♥rt* formula to create a safe place to clear the unwanted past, uncomfortable memories of hurt and emotional pain and re-connect with our own open heart that nurtures self-worth and self-love. While living with this connection of confidence we can trust in the universal plan for us – letting go of our control and attachment to past and future because God's plan is better than ours.
Your presence is such a gift!

Remember

where you were
where you are now

and

Trust

where you will be.

CHAPTER NINE

The Inner Relationship/Connection with the Beloved Experience

You are whole on your own, and the completion of the beloved experience is knowing yourself and inspiring your partner to be all that they are.

I KNOW WHO I AM
AND
IN YOUR EYES

I SEE
ALL THAT I AM

Become the beloved to attract and inspire the beloved relationship

When we begin to feel the beloved experience, we have learned to live without judgment and blame. We have taken responsibility for the love we have inside or the lack of love we feel. By using the *Pocket Guide to your He♥rt* formula, we can create a shift in perception so that we can connect with our inner peace with another.

Connect with your truth and your pure love in relationship to feel safe from within and to open your heart. We sometimes forget who we are and what we desire for ourselves in relationship. We can become the good little boys and girls for the love we desire, for the comfortable experience outside of us. All we need is self-love and the inner connection embraces our self-worth, allowing us to BE IN LOVE, to live our life without conditions or neediness, creating the most important relationship – with ourselves.

Fall in love and live in love...
Your heart is waiting.

Your little girl/boy is a symbol of your past and your emotions. When you take care of your emotional body, you connect with your emotions by using the symbol of childhood.

Mary Anne learned to live connected to her open heart and self-love. She cleared her past resentments and hurts and is now more present and peaceful. When people meet her, they ask, "Who is the new man in your life?" She doesn't have a new man, and she responds, "It's the new me!" Mary Anne is feeling her own love.

I have also experienced this in myself, walking with a skip in my stride and a sparkle in my eye when I was in a new relationship. We know what that feels like ... the ignition of romantic love. If we can learn this on our own, we can look and feel more attractive to others. Everyone wants to be near us to feel it, to know it, even though they have it in themselves, waiting to be connected. Mary Anne is living differently and feeling her own love inside. She has attracted her beloved.

CHAPTER TEN

The Little Boy and The Little Girl

It fascinates me to see how we all dance in relationship in similar ways. Aspects of every love story break-up or dysfunction can be recognized in our own lives.

I have experienced my heart shutting down or getting turned off when a man in my life behaves like the little boy, needy for love, or the bad little boy, guilty and afraid that he will not be loved. Yes, it can be a turn off, but shutting down your own heart will only create a separation between you. While he is feeling his wound from childhood, he is looking for approval or love. When you shut down, you become his mother who is disappointed and denying him love in that moment.

Can you choose to not judge him and allow him the opportunity to remember who he is? He needs to take care of himself, feel his own love inside, instead of waiting for someone else to fix him and make it better.

Connecting to your own open heart creates a wonderful reflection. When he is not connected to his self-worth, remember who he is because he does not remember himself in that moment. Connect to the truth and reflect your self-worth.

I have found myself feeling my needy little girl or bad girl in relationship. When the man at the time triggered this feeling in me, I felt unloved or not good enough.

When a woman finds herself in this place she might want the man to fix her or take care of her. Her lack of self-worth might be triggered because she feels his disappointment or anger. This behavior is a turn-off to men and they may shut down or emotionally leave. There may not be a safe place for truth, intimacy or making love. The little girl inside is looking for her father's love. Most men get tired of fathering their partners, although in some cases a man might enjoy this role because it makes him feel good, or he enjoys the power that control gives him. This is also unattractive and a turn-off in relationship. Instead of abandoning his partner emotionally, he could create a safe place for her to feel her fears. The woman in the relationship must make it clear that she is not his mother when he asks for emotional support. The man is not the father in the relationship and must respect and honor her as a woman, even if she is vulnerable or in fear.

Meditation for the Inner Relationship

Connect with your inner child …
be the loving parent to him/her.

Connect with your full heart …
feel your extraordinary SELF.

Visualize your bridge…this safe, beautiful place in nature. Get comfortable as you breathe deeply, connecting with the emotions triggered in the moment.

See your little girl/boy (you when you were young) on the bridge with you.

Create a safe place for your child to feel … unloved … disappointment … fear … anger … resentment … jealousy … lack … not good enough … whatever the feelings, allow them to be embraced by knowing they are there … feel the discomfort.

Hold your child … take care of him/her.

Talk to your partner on the bridge and express all of your feelings. Tell them how you feel and use your partner to talk about it … here on the bridge.

Cut the emotional cord and re-connect with your own love. Hold your child and feel the love and support…the protection. Be the love …

Look into your partner's eyes, or into the eyes of the one you are uncomfortable with, and feel your own open heart … feel your strength and self-worth.

CHAPTER ELEVEN

The Mother/Father Dance

Case Study: ***Beth and Paul***
Issues: Love of Mother/Father

The needy love in women represents the little girl wanting her father's love. Beth lived daily with emotional abuse from her husband Paul. His disapproval, control and lies tormented her and shut her down. She lost her voice and couldn't say, "I'm out of here." Each time Beth stood up for herself, he abused her more. She lived in fear.

Beth felt like she was in a concentration camp, a prison where she could only act as Paul wanted her to and dress a certain way to please him. She felt she had lost her identity. Beth had come to Canada, met her husband while she was on a trip, and ended up moving from Europe to live with him. During the romantic stage of the relationship she ignored the signs of control and she became pregnant and preoccupied. The love and attention that Paul gave her initially was enough and created a safe place for her here in Canada. But having left her family and friends she eventually began to feel her aloneness. Her lonely heart started to shut down and Paul's dominant personality and disrespectful attitude became worse. She couldn't talk on the phone with her friends, he wouldn't allow her to have friends over, and when she did he would be rude, driving them away. Beth's only feeling of love was with her child who she filled up, shutting down more and more from her husband.

So when she started to give her love to the baby boy, Paul became jealous and started projecting all of his anger and lack of love on Beth, blaming her for everything. She shut down her love to Paul and he blamed her. The self-hatred created a toxic home. Beth became more homesick and isolated. The *Pocket Guide to your He♥rt* formula helped Beth find her voice and open her own heart.

Beth spent a year finding the safe place in her and eventually stopped blaming Paul. She was able to talk to him about her feelings and she stood up for herself. Paul continued to blame her, however, and she had no choice but to go back home with her little boy.

A lot of people get hurt when they don't know how to communicate and sometimes it might be too late. Whatever choice you make is the right choice for you.

Beth shut down and stopped connecting with her Goddess. Beth blamed Paul because he wasn't filling her up and he became her father who shut down his love from her. Paul couldn't make her happy. Beth had never received the love from her father and she created the same experience with Paul. Beth continues to find her own self-love so that she doesn't attract the same relationship type.

Case Study: *Lori*
Issues: **Mother/Father**

Lori never felt the love from her mother, but her father filled her up with love. Lori was her father's light and love and giving to her filled him up. Lori's father did everything he could to make her happy and Lori's mother resented the attention her husband gave to their daughter. This experience caused Lori's mother to shut down, feeling jealous and not good enough. Lori felt her mother close down while growing up and this created anger and resentment in her. Lori's mother was no different – her anger and resentment shut her heart down.

As a woman, Lori could never find a man that would fill her up enough. She would eventually be disappointed and shut down with her boyfriends. Lori became her mother.

Each relationship reinforced the void in her and Lori realized the void was her lack of self-love. The Inner Workout took her to a place of anger and resentment, disappointment and pain in all her relationships. As she released her anger with her mother she saw how the shut-down was in both of them. She let go of blaming her mother and forgave her. Lori connected with her own life force and open heart. When she brought her dad onto the bridge she visualized the relationship with him and saw that he gave so much to her in order to get love. Lori was his light and she saw how needy he was. She expected her father to fill her up to feel the love. She let go of this perception and she cut the cord from her father. Lori re-connected with her own compassionate, loving heart, as she let go of both her mother and father. Lori felt the space where the emotions of fear and lack lived (void of love) and she felt her own love and energy move through her body. Lori felt full on her own and free to attract a relationship that was not going to have to fill her up or shut her down.

Lori continued to heal issues with her mother and father as she danced differently with the new man in her life … he was the reflection of her healed heart.

> ***Show me your mother's face I will tell you who you are. I know his father, how do you expect me not to know him.*** Kahlil Gibran – *The Prophet*

It doesn't matter what we have on our agenda for finding our mates, we will attract our mother or father energy and experience if we have not taken the time to heal that part of us, to see them in us and accept it. No matter what our parents were like, or how hard they tried, they did the best they could and might not have known how to feel their own love. Once you realize that you've attracted the same energy as your parents', you can find a way to heal and let go.

When in relationship or looking for a relationship, you can use conflicts and uncomfortable people to heal your past attachment to your mother or father. Know that the love is in you. It was not up to your parents to fill you up. The inspiration of self-love is a wonderful gift we can give to our children and partners. We take the painful journey of longing for what is already there and we re-create the experience of the void that we felt as children. Re-connect with the love inside and inspire your life.

Love is like death, it changes everything.

I believe that when we end a relationship and we take responsibility for our part, we may be ending that part of our wounded self in relationship. Physically the relationship is over and emotionally the attachment to the mother/father dance is over. We can then birth fully into the relationship within and feel more self-worth and self-love. We may have to leave the relationship because the other person has not let go of the mother/father dance that stops the joy and love between us expanding.

If we have not taken responsibility for our own soul's lesson at the end of the relationship, then the relationship may still live in our bodies. Release the past and the experience with this person by taking responsibility and letting go.

I feel that what I didn't know brought me to the experiences, issues and suppressed emotions that I had to feel in order to know what I know now. The struggle was that I didn't know then how to let go in a healthy way – to let go of my pain, anger and resentments and to let go of fear.

We tend to attract partners that trigger old wounds with our parents. If we can stay in a relationship and heal our own issues before we move on, there can be the opportunity for our next relationship to open and deepen, instead of react or shut down as in the past.

If you can heal your mother/father dance, by using these relationships and this formula, you can be free to be in a beloved experience. This moment of freedom has no attachments to fear. You are safe to be all that you are, in your darkness and in your highest vibration.

Meditation with Father/Mother

Breathe deeply as you visualize your bridge. Feel each step as you walk towards a door at the end of the bridge. Be aware of what surrounds you … unconditionally loving nature.

Open the door and see yourself when you were a child (4-8 yrs). Take his/her hand and feel the safe union as you walk together to the home you were raised in. If you do not remember your home, you can invite your parents to meet you on the bridge.

Find your mother … which room is she in? Spend time with her and feel your emotions as you remember her. Is she shut down? Did she give you love? Did you feel hurt…shut down…resentment?…If she wasn't available or if she passed on you may feel the void…did you feel good enough?…Whatever you feel, allow the words to help you release past suppressed truth. Let it all out…cry if you need to…scream…feel them…feel you.

See the emotional cord connecting you to your mother and when you are ready, count 1, 2, 3…

Cut the cord and hold your little girl/boy. Stand in front of your mother and feel your compassionate heart. You don't need her love or approval…you have your own. Stand in front of her and feel your own love.

Inspire your mother, here on the bridge. Take care of your own inner child, hold him/her and feel the unconditional love...feel the peace as you let go of the perception that it was up to your mother or father to give you your love. If they were not connected to their own power of love and if they were needy or resentful, they couldn't give the love to you. They didn't know how to love you in a healthy way.

Repeat the same process with your father. Feel any suppressed emotions as you sit beside him. If you feel your void, disconnect from the perception that your father is the reflection of your void of love. If you don't feel good enough or if you feel his disappointment, let go of the disappointment that you have for them or yourself.

Feel your fears and your anger...use your father to heal your self-worth issues.

Once you use your Mother/Father to release any emotions, truth or past experiences with your parents that are uncomfortable, make sure you re-connect with your open forgiving heart.

- The Inner Relationship – connecting with you when you were a child.
- The Inner Workout – use your Mother/Father to feel the unloving truth within. Let your parents go emotionally.
- Inner Peace – connect with your own loving strength, and self-approval. Take responsibility and grow up.

Inspire Your Relationship

Inspire your relationship and live what you desire. Some of my friends tell me I'm so lucky that Bruce is so loving and honoring. It's all in how we give and receive from our own connection to ourselves. For example, once I gave a friend a foot massage. I felt full in my heart; there were no conditions. It felt just as comfortable for me to rub her feet as it would be for her to rub mine. I have regular massages from my husband or professionals and I know how wonderful it feels. I sometimes rub my own feet when they need it, taking care of myself. I started to rub her feet and she melted into the experience of enjoying it. She said, "I've never had my feet rubbed by someone else, other than a massage therapist." I asked her, "Have you ever rubbed anyone else's feet?" Her response was, "No." I then asked, "Do you ever rub your own feet?" Again she replied, "No."

Take care of yourself and love with no attachments or conditions and you will receive it all back. Give to another and to yourself the loving action that you yearn for.

Some women in relationship whine about their emptiness, blaming their partners. They're tired of giving and not receiving. Take a look at how you give. Are you a victim, giving from your void or from your lack? The experience can be received or felt with attachments and resentments, or felt with a heart that is needy for love … A TURN OFF! The shut-down is felt and the inauthenticity is there within the action. If you feel empty of love, your partner may not be able to fill your void.

I have seen many cases with both men and women, where neither can ever feel satisfied. For the man, it may have been the mother who gave, gave and gave, filling him up with attention, things and love. He was her world, her love, and he became the good little boy for mommy's love. So he is constantly looking for a woman who is going to fill him up in that way. For a woman, it could be the same experience with the mother or father, usually the father, who has filled his daughter up because he does not feel the love from his wife. The wife may not be in touch with her connection to self-love and may not feel the love from her husband. By the father filling the daughter with attention, love and things for love, he detaches from his wife. The wife usually becomes more shut down, perhaps even jealous, because her husband is not giving enough to her.

Little girls may grow up into women looking for love from men, looking for the man to fill them up. The man eventually becomes exhausted because it's never enough. The little girl who is now a woman, has not learned to give to herself … attracting the experience of the void in the relationship. This void in her may attract a man who will eventually abandon her or disappoint her. He will feel his own wound of not being good enough and both may shut down from one another. In this dance, each person has the opportunity to feel their own void/lack of self-love/self-worth and to help the other to heal.

Put the other person on the bridge and speak to them the truth about what is missing, how you feel about them and what isn't good enough.

TELL THEM HOW YOU FEEL! FEEL, LET GO.

Re-connect to your own source of love and power.

Case Study: ***Janice and Ted***
Issues: Judgement, Criticism, Lack of Self-Love

When Janice came to see me she really had no idea why she was so shut down. She didn't know what it was like to feel any emotions, love or pain. When she looked back on her marriage that was in separation, she remembered how she felt about Ted, her ex-husband. She really didn't like him, she was closed to making love with him and she didn't want him to touch her. Janice could feel herself shut down and she didn't feel sexual with him. Her heart was closed over the years and she blamed him for everything uncomfortable in her life. Ted eventually was unfaithful in the marriage, which gave her the opening to leave.

Janice worked through her process by using the Inner Workout, releasing a lot of suppressed anger and control. She saw how she controlled her emotions and shut down her heart. Janice felt her anger with him and how she never felt good enough. She saw how she attracted a man like her father – he had the same energy – angry, shut down and judgmental, which was a turn-off to her. Janice recognized how she became the reflection of him as she became shut down, judgmental and critical, suppressing her anger.

Janice then used Ted to feel all of her anger and lack of self-love. She put him on the bridge and she felt, she cried and she opened to the truth of her own suppressed past pain. Janice felt her self-hatred and how she blamed him for feeling not good enough.

JANICE LET GO AS SHE USED TED TO FEEL! SHE CUT THE EMOTIONAL CORD

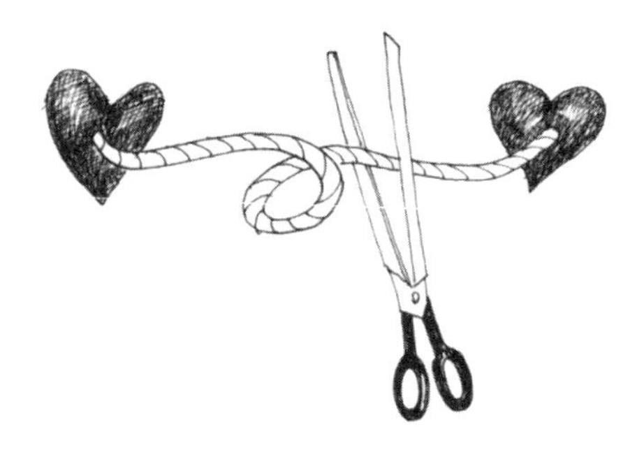

THAT HELD ON TO THE PAIN AND BLAME. JANICE FORGAVE TED, LET GO AND RE-CONNECTED TO HER SELF-LOVE AS SHE FELT HER HEART OPEN. SHE FORGAVE TED AS SHE REALIZED SHE NEVER NEEDED HIS LOVE AND APPROVAL. JANICE FELT COMPASSION.

Janice recognized all the parts of her father in Ted that reflected her dark side. She told her dark side (the aspects of herself that she did not love), how much she hated it and didn't want this in her body. She visualized her victim and she screamed at her, telling her off. Janice didn't want to be that anymore and she didn't want to feel this connection. She saw how she shut her heart down to herself, and she felt the pain. She had abandoned her own love when she shut down. Janice found compassion for the little girl who felt unloved and who felt the disapproval. She felt the abandonment of her mother who died when she was young. She cried and grieved and then cut the cord with both her mother and father. Janice was free to open her heart as she forgave her mom, dad and Ted. This was the beginning of her new-found *feeling gland* and self-love.

Each relationship of struggle can bring up in us:

The Pocket Guide to your He♥rt formula can take you to a healthy relationship of love with your self and another.

Feel your own connection to:

Self-Love

Self-Worth

Self-Awareness

Truth and Open Heart

Peace

The first time you experience your partner's wounds and issues is like the first time you experience your parents' anger or fear and pain as a child. I didn't know how to be with my past relationships when they were feeling their uncomfortable issues and emotions. Now I know how to take care of my own wounded self *instead of plugging into my partner's pain. If I had only known how, there might have been an opening, a chance for love. If I had only known what to do.*

Living the beloved experience is being available when the other person slips into self-doubt and lack of self-love. We cannot be there emotionally if we only know how to plug into each other, blaming, judging or being the victim. When we take care of our emotional pain and are connected to all that we are, we can do it differently. A daily practice is important to keep you emotionally fit and present to be available for your loved ones. Self-love and self-care allows you to be available in love and authentic in truth. It allows the safeness to be experienced from within you, creating a safe place of comfort in your home, in your relationships, in your family.

CHAPTER TWELVE

Holding the Space for Your Partner

What does this mean?

Issues will come up, emotions will be felt and we will trigger one another. Life will create stress and dysfunction. When our partner is out of control or feeling miserable, can we allow them the space and time to feel? Can we keep our heart open and create a safe place for them to allow their emotions to move through them?

Holding the space means not judging. A compassionate heart can reflect the truth. Kindness can embrace the experience and if you don't panic or try to fix the other person, the solution usually emerges in the safe arms of the relationship. Commitment and trust in each other at a time of fear can be felt if one person can remember the truth and love. When our partner is feeling lack, can we hold the space and allow the uncomfortable experience to release the fear?

I believe that if we are awake in our relationship, we can feel our lover's pain and we can hold the space as they move through it.

Each night Bruce and I give each other the opportunity to unlock the door within to express our feelings.

Our experiences are personal and may seem silly and dramatized or overly sensitive sometimes, but we try not to judge, fix or say *I told you so* or *I know better.*

When we hold the space we also create a safe place for one another to unload if we need to, trying not to take anything personally and sometimes, in our humanness, it can be hard. We may shut down. Practice makes perfect for us.

CHAPTER THIRTEEN

The Inner Workout

Things that I didn't know created the experiences that have helped me find greater understanding. I struggled before I learned to let go and re-connect to my own love. Letting go is a lifelong journey.

Letting go
of attachment
of my plan
of anger and resentment
of fear
of guilt
of the PAST

If we are willing to let go of our past over and over again, we will experience growth and change. We then can attract someone who reflects the connection to self-love, self-worth and peace. The Inner Workout is the part of the formula that helps you feel and let go!

Go inside you
Where truth lives

Out of the prison of your mind
Find the space in your heart.

Once you have released the negativity from a past relationship, it is truly wonderful to look at the positives. These are all opportunities of attracting a positive experience in our life because we know it and we feel it. Let's not forget the beauty and the love that we did feel in the relationship at times and know that the love that we felt was also our own love.

See your beloved through the eyes of love
Without judgment
Understand that, at times, they will not feel love
Remember who they are
when they are feeling their darkness
Be the reflection of love.

By taking care of our emotions on a daily basis, we can detach from our past, re-connect with ourselves and live more present. When we are more present in the moment, we can live more present in relationship.

Our suppressed emotions and unresolved issues from our past keep us disconnected from our peace. The more peace that we connect with, the more space we will have, because we have released suppressed emotions and experiences from relationships we have carried around in us. Once this burden has been released and we have more space, our self-worth rises to a higher vibration and we can feel more love.

We don't have to react inappropriately because we will not be triggered.

If you have had relationships that had to end, take the time to process the truth of the experience and the emotions by putting the person on the bridge. Visualize the bridge and see this person. Feel the truth, the pain, the resentment, the blame and feel the anger or the fear, the self-doubt or the void of love.

See the attachment to this person with all of your uncomfortable emotions, visualizing the emotional cord connecting you. Count to three and cut the cord. You can now release the experience and this person. Re-connect with your own source of love, breathing fully and feeling your own energy that ignites you. Allow your breath to lift the energy up into your body. Open your heart as you forgive this person. You don't need their love or approval anymore. Feel your open heart as you stand in front of him/her. Forgive and feel your compassionate heart. He/she was the reflection of what you needed to own ... can you continue to hold yourself in this place of emotional pain?

Allow the relationships to trigger the emotions to create the process of feeling, letting go, forgiving and re-connecting.

Case Study: *Susie and Jeff*
Issues: Abandonment, Needing Love, Resentment

Susie felt abandoned, needy and full of pain because Jeff, the man she loved, didn't want to be in relationship with her. She felt her void of love fully as she experienced his rejection. He was closed and he ran away. Susie believed that he was the love of her life, but knew she had to let go of him. For months Susie felt her lack of self-worth and self-love. The grief of the lost relationship was painful until she learned to re-ignite her own heart and to respect herself again. Her broken heart brought her hours of tears, anger, fear and resentment. Susie used the experience to fight her way back to her own love inside. Her strength was very attractive and she started living more open. Susie still felt Jeff was the perfect partner for her, but she knew he couldn't be there and she let go of him when she let go of her pain. Susie started to feel good on her own and that's when Jeff came back to her. He proposed and within months they married.

Soon after their honeymoon, issues started to come up and Jeff blamed Susie for all of his failings. There was so much love in the partnership that it was now his turn to feel his lack. Jeff blamed Susie until one day she risked losing him again and stood up to him, saying, "If you don't take care of your own issues and take responsibility for yourself I cannot stay with you." Susie told him to stop blaming her or the relationship was over. Jeff didn't want to lose her and this forced him to finally take responsibility. Jeff had a lot of suppressed anger because of unresolved issues with his dad. As he felt his past, he moved into a healthier heart, instead of blaming or shutting down. This experience gave them another opportunity to love more deeply.

It's very possible for one person in relationship to start the process of self-discovery and healing, shifting the whole relationship. We can't fix another, but we can inspire them.

One person can change a dance step and this movement can create the opening. With this opening there is an opportunity for the strength of love to overpower the fear.

Susie and Jeff are now living the beloved experience together.

Be The User

Use your relationship to heal your wounded self. Use the relationship to see the mother/father dance that is being experienced and heal this aspect of your hurt child within.

Any relationship can be the gift that opens your heart to truth.

We continue to be triggered by the same relationship issues until we see ourselves reflected in them. The part in us that shuts down reacts, withdraws, denies our own love, feels guilty, angry or not good enough and resentful.

All of these triggers stop us from loving fully. Face your fear of not being loved and take a risk.

STOP BLAMING AND START OWNING!!
SURRENDER AND RESPECT OURSELVES AND OTHERS

It Comes From Nowhere

It comes from nowhere
This sadness … such a heaviness
Yesterday I felt fine, on top of the world.
Is it the cloudy dark day?
I am having trouble breathing fully …
My heart is in pain …
It comes from nowhere …
I visualize him …
He was from long ago.
He couldn't be with me
Is it you I feel?
I visualize him …
He was the one who ignored me …
Is it you again that haunts me?
I feel him …
The one that said goodbye.
My heart feels the hurt … like it is happening today.
Is it you who lied, who betrayed me …
Dishonoring the love.
I am mad … I am mad. I scream
I feel angry …
As I cry I say to you "It was not good enough."
For me, it was not good enough.
I let go another piece of past pain.
You were ready to show your face again,
So that I could heal this place in me
It came from nowhere …
I feel peace,
it comes from somewhere … in me.

Colleen Hoffman Smith

Visualize the bridge and use him/her, confronting them on the bridge ... the safe place to release the truth of what you feel. Let go and re-connect with your own open heart. Your Inner Workout with your feelings can create healthier communication.

CONFRONTATION IS EMBRACED WITH ANGER, RESENTMENT AND .... FEAR

No one enjoys confrontation because of the energy and toxic emotions that embrace the words. When you clear your own suppressed anger, resentment and fear, you can then communicate your feelings without blame, judgment or resentment. Healthy communication can empower the other person to hear what you need to say.

You can go on the bridge and confront all of the suppressed issues and the toxic emotions living in you that are triggered by this person. Use these people, by visualizing them in front of you on the bridge. Clear the heaviness of your emotions that close your heart, all of the feelings and truth that stop you from being authentic and attractive. They will never know! BE THE USER! SPEAK TO THEM, YELL, CRY, ON THE BRIDGE.

Can you BE, instead of being right? When people fight, each trying to prove the other wrong, the engaging can create a place where they become obsessed with their own belief system, not opening to another's opinion.

Can you believe in yourself enough to let go of being right or the need for someone to say that you are right? Our need for love and approval may be the reason why we shut down when someone dishonors us. We may be afraid to say no or tell the truth because we don't want the rejection. Create a safe loving relationship with yourself.

I see my parents in love and more at peace with each other now.

What has shifted between them?

They no longer blame each other; they don't need to be right.

Stay emotionally fit with a daily practice.

Our Wounded Self

Each one of us carries our past emotional wounds. This wound can ooze and open when confronted with the energy of the same experience that brings up our lack of love. Every relationship or experience that brings up the same void in us can trigger us to shut down part of our heart, creating walls like armor. We are all energy and when we feel someone in our space or in our life who has suppressed anger or who projects anger, shuts down or abandons us, creating the experience of fear … our wound may respond and open.

Physical, emotional or sexual abuse leaves a memory in our bodies that creates deep scars. A client once told me that she remembers being picked up out of her bed and thrown across the room many nights as she was growing up. Another client was a young boy with deep wounds because he was sexually molested by priests. Other clients have come to me knowing that they were abused, but not remembering the details, only the feeling. We have all experienced, as children, the projection of shut-down or anger and remember how uncomfortable we felt.

There are different levels of memories and wounds. I know women who, as children, were abandoned by their fathers, molested sexually by their grandfathers, and then emotionally and physically abandoned and betrayed by their husbands. Abandonment is a huge wound that could come from the memory of the cold, shut-down of a mother's heart when she didn't know how to feel her own love, or show it, or the unavailability of one or both parents. Experiences of separation, feeling the void inside because of a death of a father or mother or the yearning for a relationship that we've never had are other examples of abandonment. Some people may look for love, peace and relationships their entire lives, without understanding what they are truly looking for.

Abuse, on any level, is emotionally painful. Many people do not realize that it existed in their past until they start attracting abuse in their adult life. *The experience or relationship can be the pathway to healing.* You can recognize it when you have attracted a partner who becomes violent or verbally abusive. This relationship is an opportunity to go deep within and find a way to stand up for yourself. To go beyond your fear of losing the love and not allow this abuse in your life, so that you can show your children that it is not healthy.

This experience may take you to your lack of self-love and self-worth. Become aware and use the inner workout as you visualize your abuser and stay with your feelings, expressing them fully! Process with these feelings by standing up and saying, "No, I don't want this in my life anymore! I don't need your love or approval! I don't need your abuse! I don't need you to be the reminder of my void! I do not need to be abandoned!"

Cut the emotional cord from this person and let go, move into your root chakra (the base of your spine) and feel your life force. Remember all the love that you have and allow it to open your heart again. Forgive this soul if you can. LET GO! You may never forgive the behavior, because no child should ever be put through abuse. No one should dishonor or disrespect you at any age. I do not know if we can fully heal the wound, but we can change our perception about ourselves and feel the truth of the present. Give yourself gentleness and self-protection.

The BREAKTHROUGH is letting go of past

and the opening of your heart for yourself

There is a movie called *Bliss*, about a man and a woman who get married. He starts noticing that she is obsessed with cleaning the house and she tells him that she fakes her lovemaking. Her behavior confuses him because he believes that she is the most sexual being he knows and that they have a healthy love life. He starts feeling her shut-down and realizes something is wrong so he starts following her, thinking that she's going to meet another man. The man turns out to be a sex therapist and the wife will not talk about it when he confronts her. So he meets the therapist and confronts him. The therapist explains to him that his wife has terrible abuse issues from childhood and the truth is that she really loves her husband, but her past is affecting her and she is shutting down emotionally and sexually. The wife was molested sexually as a child by her father and the childhood abuse was the root of many of her problems. The husband begs the therapist to teach him how to help her heal. The therapist says, "I will teach you how to love from your heart and not your penis." The husband loves his wife so much that he changes his own perception and creates a safe place for her. He has personal sessions with the sex therapist each day as this wise teacher shares his wisdom.

The woman had a lot of suppressed anger and fear and you can see in the movie that she pretends to be the good little girl, not only for her father but also her husband. She cannot sustain it any longer and starts to go insane. This film has an amazing truthfulness and positive outcome. Their deep love became the healing foundation for their future.

Use your relationship to feel what you need to own, either lack of commitment to self or your own void of self-love and self-worth. Take this person on your bridge and feel them in front of you. Tell them how you feel … the truth. Let go – re-connect with your own heart.

DO YOU NEED THIS EXPERIENCE ANY LONGER? IS IT IMPORTANT ENOUGH?

DO YOU NEED TO BEHAVE LIKE THIS ANY LONGER? ASK YOURSELF THE QUESTION … "AM I TAKING CARE OF MYSELF IN THIS RELATIONSHIP?"

Where Is My Beloved?

Where is my beloved? I want a partner. I hear this from women and men, yearning for a relationship. I remember this feeling and the uncomfortable empty cry from within. I feel the difference now, knowing I am fine on my own, yet still desiring partnership. This is more authentic and more attractive, unlike the needy desperation I had before. I knew I *wanted* a partner!

I have seen how some men and women, as soon as they feel uncomfortable and driven by their need to feel ignited, say, "Next!". As soon as the love brings up the feelings, they run, not wanting to face their own issues. A lot of people in relationships look for someone else, or think there is someone better, instead of being fully in the relationship and taking responsibility by looking at themselves within the partnership. If you are always looking over your shoulder, the distraction and disconnection can cause a great void in the relationship, including non-commitment, unavailability, lack of interest and unsafeness, leading to fear and self-worth issues.

The process of self-discovery can open your own awareness and can become the practical exercise to feel your own separation within.

Listen to your heart and your body. If you start feeling uncomfortable, take the time to be with whatever you are feeling. Get to know people and see their uniqueness.

Allow each experience and each person to be an opportunity to get to know more of yourself.

CHAPTER FOURTEEN

Fear

Fear can keep us humble and open. Be aware and present with fear so that you can work with it. Try not to hide from it or push it away. Fear can come from anywhere, when we least expect it – the sound of someone's voice or an unexpected experience can suddenly bring out our fear. BE WITH IT.

If the fear in another or in the relationship is stronger than the love in the relationship, it can be destructive. Instead of mirroring the fear, hold the space so that it can be talked about and released. Fear can shut us down, keep us stuck and even destroy the relationship. One of the challenges in our lives is facing it. Any experience that is not of love is usually fear-based. Do we spend our days running away from or denying the feeling of fear? Life reveals it in many ways. Can we face them and deal with the challenges life presents?

Instead of reacting we can take action by asking ourselves, "Am I taking care of myself right now?"

When our partner is feeling fear, instead of hooking into them, can we be open to feeling our own fear? Know in this moment that they do not love and accept themselves. Be the reflection of NO FEAR.

If they judge you or project their fear onto you, it's not up to you to fix them.

Take care of yourself, parent yourself, and stand in open heart. This action can remind others of who they are – be the reflection of love.

Disappointment and Disapproval

A Gentle/man Facing Punishment

I have several male clients who have come to me ready to leave their relationships. They may feel that their partner disrespects them and projects anger, blaming them for everything. The man has come to me feeling battered emotionally; the wife is angry and shut down and she punishes him constantly. He feels there is nothing he can do that is good enough. They both feel they are being judged and are disappointed with each other. They are worn down and at their darkest place within.

Each one of these men is a gentle man, very loving, wanting only to be loved in return. They do everything they can to keep life peaceful. They have lost touch with themselves and have reached a point where they want to leave the marriage but don't have the courage. They are living in fear even though they have already left the relationship emotionally.

The process of self-awareness helped them realize how they allowed the relationship to shut down their own love. They take action by releasing the resentment and suppressed emotions they have pushed aside, by visualizing their wife on the bridge, feeling and speaking the truth. Once they detach from their wife or partner who has such power over them, they find an inner strength to live more authentically.

The Inner Workout takes them to their own self-hatred instead of blaming their partner. Each time they find their way to their open heart they realize that they have allowed someone else to tell them they were less than whole. This re-connection to their self-worth empowers them to stand up and say, "It's not good enough. I want love and peace in my life."

Bit by bit they release their resentment. Each of the men I had sessions with started to have a voice. They didn't want to tolerate emotional abuse and started to feel their compassionate heart.

The man who experiences the feeling of his little boy may see with clarity that his past experience with his mother was one of abandoned love, disappointment or projection of anger with disapproval. His mother might have been shut down or miserable and as a boy he learned to walk on eggshells around her. These men felt the same issues in their present relationship and saw the opportunity to heal their childhood perception that they were not good enough. Their mothers were no different than their wives, not knowing the connection of self-love; they had learned their misbehavior as little girls.

What can you do?

These men took their mothers onto the bridge to get to their feelings of anger and resentment. I guided them to say things like, "You didn't love me" or "You didn't give me love." Feeling the shut-down and expressing their hurt, feeling the void with their mother, they realized that all of these emotions were the same as those experienced with their wives. By letting go and cutting the emotional cord, they could then release their past suppressed feelings and re-connect with their own source of love, finding their way to their compassionate heart as they forgave their mothers and their wives for not knowing how to love them. When we heal with our mothers and fathers, we can attract and experience our partner differently.

Courage

Once you live with a healthy connection to your own heart, not shut down or in fear, you can create the opportunity for healing with your partner while communicating and sharing from a safe place in you.

A few of the wives of these men became aware of the shift in their husbands and they started to take responsibility for their part in the relationship. The courage of their partner inspired them to want to find their own pathway to the beloved relationship. I have experienced couples who have shifted into healing loving relationships as they change their dance step and found self-awareness, self-acceptance and gentle love. I celebrate them!!

It's very hard for a man to make love to his "mother." So I speak to all of the women who are reading this book. If you start to punish, criticize, shut down, withdraw or scold your husband, he may eventually see you as his mother and the intimacy and openness could disappear. Your partner desires the Goddess.

The process described in this chapter can also result from the same behavior by men. If a husband or partner is shut down, controlling or critical, his behavior can trigger the father dance with the woman. Eventually the woman may shut down, feel angry and her fear will close her heart or she will leave, sometimes finding love in another man's arms. A woman who is not safe with her partner may feel closed emotionally and the fear will create barriers in the relationship and stop the flow of open love.

FEAR stops the FLOW

YOU ARE WORTHY OF LOVE

SELF-LOVE HEALS AND GIVES YOU

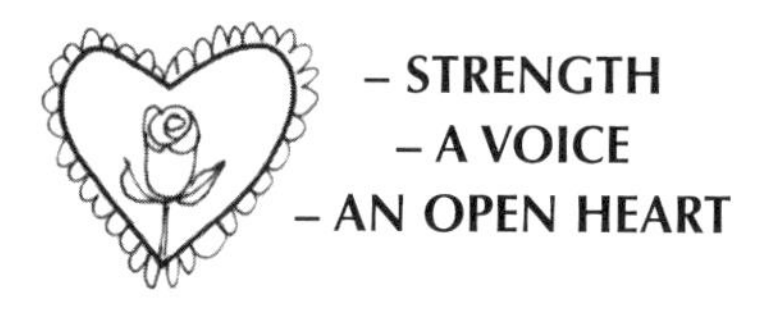

CHAPTER FIFTEEN

Anger and Resentment

I fear the tyrant approaching me with the sweet voice so that he may later rule me with the strength of his arms.

Kahlil Gibran – *The Prophet*

This line speaks to the truth of how we can be lured by the tyrant, whose need to find the love is as strong as the victim's, each one reflecting the void of love.

Our problems, issues and wounds can become the toxicity of a relationship.

Criticism, Judgment, Negativity

Criticism is another expression of our own self-hatred and self-loathing projected on another.

This experience is our own lack of self-worth if we have attached the notion of who we are to what someone else thinks of us. To criticize is a no-no! It can destroy and cause the death of love.

Criticism is judging another, and when we are criticized we feel judged.

These uncomfortable behaviors are fear-based and it is the fear that drives us to misbehavior, hurting others or staying in the relationship and being hurt. Using this formula and releasing our past attachments to our lack of self-love can strengthen our self-worth so that we don't have to criticize or judge another person or stay and be criticized or judged.

The Spider

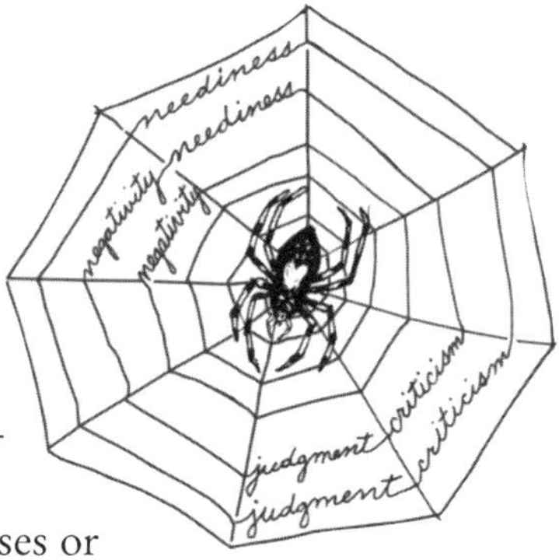

We have all experienced the personal web of a human spider – either the creative weaving of our life patterns with positive opportunities for progress into new phases or the negative side that can trap us, trying to bring us down with the stickiness of criticism and destructiveness. We can be the spider or we can attract the spider … either way, the experience is for us.

Weave your life opportunities with conscious relationships. Try not to get caught up in the web of criticism, judgment, negativity and neediness.

Anger

I believe that love dies when the relationship is poisoned with the toxic energy of anger that is projected or anger that is shut down.

We all have anger; it's part of our human experience. But how do we take care of anger? Some people say that yelling and expressing it is healthy, but it isn't. Shutting down and pushing aside our anger is not healthy either. Anger is toxic to our relationships, our children, family and co-workers. We can use our anger in a healthy way if we use it to take action, change direction, or stand up for ourselves. If we project it or suppress it, we're either abusing another or ourselves. Anger in a relationship will eventually cause separation and anger in our heart will cause illness.

Anger Management

The Inner Workout is a fantastic process to deal with our anger on a daily basis. Once we release our suppressed resentments, we can feel a lot more open and connect to the present moment and the person we are experiencing. Each person who agitates us can be the one we bring onto the bridge and use to release our anger. Take responsibility and use this tool to create a healthier life.

Inner Workout for Anger

Quiet your mind as you connect with your breath. Be aware of your breathing, relaxing into the gentleness of your inner relationship.

Visualize your bridge, seeing nature surrounding you. See yourself walking on your bridge … be conscious of what is around you. Create a safe place, a comfortable experience, as you see yourself as a child. Hold him/her and feel the safe love as you re-connect.

Invite the person who is making you feel angry onto the bridge. Feel your anger as you stand in front of him/her.

Speak the truth of all that you feel; be aware of what you need to say. Unlock the resentment and feel the anger. Your words will open you and you may speak out loud.

Scream, cry and release all of your inner truth.

See the emotional cord connected to this person. You don't need them to be responsible for your anger. Count to three …ONE … TWO … THREE … and CUT THE CORD.

Re-connect with your own source…connect to your root chakra and feel your power. Move into yourself and your energy and open your heart as you stand before this person who triggers your anger. Forgive him/her and feel your heart open. Feel your love as you let him/her go. Be the inspiration of peace as you feel your inner strength and love.

Use people and experiences here on your bridge to release your anger and resentments. You can then speak clearly and firmly if you need to stand up for yourself. Anger may shut you down or push you off your center. Use your anger in a healthy way and release it.

Case study: ***Steve and Samantha***
Issue: Anger

The husband is a corporate professional named Steve ... the wife's name is Samantha. Steve would come home from a long day at work and Samantha would berate him for not doing enough. Steve felt constantly put down, that he was never good enough. This daily experience ignited memories of his parents' disappointment while he was growing up. Steve always felt there was something wrong with him.

Samantha and Steve were together for over 20 years, living with constant unloving energy. Steve didn't want to come home and he became a workaholic. He made lots of money and created an abundant lifestyle to keep Samantha happy. For Samantha, it was never enough and Steve became distracted and unavailable. He kept leaving his own feelings and the truth of the relationship by not being there. Samantha was not connected to her own self-awareness and she projected her self-hatred and blamed Steve. Samantha believed it was healthy to project her anger, a behavior that she learned from her mother while growing up. She saw her mother treat her father exactly the same way, squashing her father's self-worth. Samantha didn't like the way her mother treated her father and she didn't want to be like her mother. Samantha's father became a belittled man, who eventually died of a broken heart.

Steve and Samantha were reliving the same life lessons and Steve was slowly dying inside. His career distracted him from discovering his truth and his emotional pain eventually created illness. The heaviness of Samantha's negative emotions filled the entire house and the whole relationship. He tried everything he could to please her and stay out of her way and he lost his own connection to self. This tough relationship brought Steve inside to feel and surrender.

Steve became aware of his emotional disconnection and he started to connect to the truth of his own shut-down. He started to take responsibility and made a healthy choice for himself. Samantha could never take any responsibility. She believed Steve was the one who was broken and she made him feel that he needed to be fixed. Eventually, with counseling, Steve left Samantha. He felt that if he stayed, he might kill himself. In fact, he was emotionally dying inside … self-destructing.

Steve finally found the strength to stand up and not deny his own personal needs … the desire for peace and love in his life. Steve is slowly letting go of blaming Samantha as he takes responsibility for his own lack of self-worth. Samantha is slowly letting go of the anger and the blame that she attached to Steve. Her life is shifting into a happier place and Steve has grown into the man he knew he could be, a loving father who is experiencing a beloved relationship with a woman. Steve found his way out … and inside himself.

He found his way out of the abuse and inside himself he found his true love … now reflected in his life.

CHAPTER SIXTEEN

Money Issues

Money fears can keep us separate from the love and faith in our hearts.

Money issues can be experienced because of a lack of money or the need to pay child support. If a husband pays child support with a lot of resentment, the experience may close his heart. If a woman does not receive child support, she may resent the lack of support. These experiences cause shut-down and resentment.

If he could get rid of the resentment and move into his open heart and if she could support herself emotionally by letting go of the resentment, the situation could be the opening to finding more love within. When the heart is open and provides the love – instead of the money representing the love – the flow of money can come back in a different way. Take a look at where your money attachments are, what the money or lack of it brings up for you. Notice if in the relationship there is any control around money. Control can block the flow of money and may create resentment in a relationship.

The feeling of deprivation or failure, of not being taken care of, or that we aren't making enough money can block us. These destructive feelings and experiences are based in fear and hooked onto our lack of self-worth. If we have money issues, we should face them and feel them. Use the bridge workout to feel and release and then talk it out with your partner instead of withholding, blaming or judging each other … find your way together.

Two hearts are better than one!

Case Study: ***Christine and Jens***
Issues: Relationship issue about money

Christine and Jens came to me for coaching. Jens was very successful professionally and he controlled all of the money in the relationship. He told Christine not to worry about money. He would take care of it. It looked like Jens was protecting and taking care of Christine, but he wanted to control the money and relationship.

Christine didn't feel a true connection and partnership with their money. Jens was the breadwinner, and he decided where the money was spent. Over time, Christine became self-aware and saw the control issues with Jens. The illusion that she was being taken care of was shattered and they were forced to face the money issues together. They blamed each other until they realized they had the choice to come together and find a solution.

Christine saw how her husband controlled everything but she had no idea that he was in financial trouble. Jens confessed that he pretended everything was great because he didn't want her not to love him. He wanted to look successful in her eyes. Christine was shocked and felt betrayed because Jens had kept this secret from her. Their financial disaster brought up many of their own personal issues and Christine chose to stand by Jens. She became more of a financial partner and he let go of his control and his fears about money within the relationship. The experience took them to truth and shifted the dance. They were able to create more intimacy with each other.

Do It Differently

Bruce and I have experienced many issues and have found safe ground to walk together. As I was expanding my book business, I needed to talk about some money issues with Bruce. I could sense that it brought up some of his fears about finances. This triggered my feelings of not being good enough. I then connected to my own worth and my own self as I felt my open heart. I didn't have to relive feelings of unworthiness or self-doubt. We flowed through the process by talking about our fears and feelings and avoided the dance of shut-down or projection. Bruce felt his fear and I didn't close my heart. We both heard one another and we let go of our past experiences. The next day there was a great opening in both of us. We had done it differently and the abundance came to support our choice of being open and not in fear.

Our wounds may not ever be totally gone, but by being able to live aware and awake if we feel betrayed or abandoned, we can stay present and not react. We do not know what levels of healing we have to go to, what more we have to feel to get to our own connection of self-worth. We might go backwards for a moment, but if we are aware of it we can take a comfortable step forward with each other and start waltzing again. Our present connection is more comfortable and centered when we take care of our past fear and resentment.

I have had many levels of intimacy where I have learned to be with myself. This process of inner connection, believing in me, respecting myself, and not betraying me is constant. Continually breathing and connecting with the source of love that I have within allows life to come to me. When I feel dishonored, disrespected, betrayed or unloved in any way, I take this opportunity to embrace the uncomfortable feelings. The perception that someone is wrong or right keeps us holding on to past pain and this arrogant expression of self-righteousness can stop the dance of intimacy. We need to be open and allow the opportunity of divine wisdom to show us the truth. Anyone can be the messenger.

CHAPTER SEVENTEEN

Secrets or Privacy

Secrets are felt energetically so it's important to share and be clear with your partner, and to be truthful with yourself. Share your fears with your partner because secrets can threaten the trust. The place from within that is holding the secret can shut down your heart and create a barrier in the relationship. It's important to keep an open flow of communication. If you are hiding something, an open heart will sense it.

Privacy is a self-honoring action, whereas a secret is embraced with fear, untruth or both. Sometimes we have experiences or feelings we want to keep private because we feel we are not safe to share the information with our partner.

I remember when I was opening to my spirituality and wanted to share it with my ex-husband. He would laugh at me or talk about it with friends in a dishonoring way. I didn't feel safe to share that part of myself with him because he would criticize, judge and mock me. So I closed off that part of me. My spirituality became my private world. Because my spirituality was so important to me, I attracted Bruce, who not only respects that part of me but also celebrates along with me the spiritual connection we have together.

The Lie is the Pea Under Your Mattress

Once you see the lie, only the truth remains. So the lie is the illusion to bring up the truth and once we see the lie, we can see the truth. Anything that feels uncomfortable can be a lie. Everything that feels good and powerful is comfortable because it comes from who we really are.

> We can feel the untruth with our partner or relationship. It will feel uncomfortable. If we are in our own untruth and have a lie living in us, our energy will be uncomfortable and can be felt. Remember the fable "*The Princess and the Pea.*"

Supplication, Softness, Inspiration

Love will bring up past pain to be healed. If you are dating someone and you feel them close, or they suddenly leave emotionally or physically, soften your heart and find your way to your own love. Their heart may have been wounded and the relationship is showing them their past and their fears. Don't try to fix them or make them comfortable. Be the reflection of an open heart by letting go of expectations and judgment. Become the understanding heart that is full already. Create a safe place for them and an opportunity for healing. They may never have experienced the openness to feel their emotions truthfully in a relationship. Inspire someone by softening yourself. If you are open, the softness of a gentle heart can be the inspiration of safe love.

Jealousy, Possession and Independence

The feeling of jealousy brings up insecurities and doubts about ourselves. If we take care of our own insecurities and self-doubt, we never have to feel jealous. We ought to feel completely safe if our husband or partner is in a room full of beautiful women. If we don't, we have to look at the issue. Talk to your partner if they project their sexual energy to others. This is dishonoring and we do not have to accept this disrespect in our lives.

Set boundaries and make it clear by standing up for yourself and respecting you! If your partner is flirting with someone, it shows a lack of respect they may not be aware of.

When men I was with flirted with other women, I usually shut down my heart and pushed aside any resentment and unloving feelings. I never talked about it because I was always told it was my problem. YES! It was my problem! Because I didn't respect myself enough to say, "No! This is not appropriate and I will not be dishonored this way."

When Bruce and I were dating, he was invited for the first time to meet my family and my sisters at my parent's 50th wedding anniversary at the cottage, a wonderful celebration. My triplet sisters Frannie and Philomene are very dynamic women. I hadn't introduced Bruce to my girlfriends yet so this was the first time I had seen him with other women. As the weekend unfolded, I started to feel uncomfortable. I could feel Bruce flirting, although I wasn't sure, but I sensed he was projecting sexual energy with my sisters. I approached him about it and he said, "Oh, you must be jealous." He dismissed my concerns and implied that it was my problem, so I let it go. But something was needling me.

After the weekend, I called my sisters and they confirmed my feelings. I called Bruce a day later and said I wanted to talk to him about the weekend. I felt I was in my open heart and I wanted to deal with the issue for my own sake. I wasn't mad at him. It was something I needed to understand and talk about with him. At this point I realized that I had felt this way many times before in other relationships when the man I was with flirted with other women, disrespecting me.

In the past I would shut down or get angry and my heart would be hurt. With Bruce I felt a lot more centered and spoke my truth with my open heart. I told him that I felt that he was projecting his sexual energy on my sisters for attention. I felt very safe talking to him, but I was not going to put up with this in any relationship ever again. I was truthful and told him my sisters were uncomfortable also. I told Bruce that sexual energy is personal and is to be shared with the person you are in relationship with. We sense when it is projected elsewhere. I know, because I used my sexual energy in the past to get attention. Men flirt and their partners shut down. Women flirt and their men are threatened and shut down or get angry.

When I explained this to Bruce he was embarrassed, not realizing he'd done such a thing. He was raised with brothers and didn't have any sisters. Bruce realized that in the past he had felt women shut down when he flirted with them. Women often feel invaded when men ogle them or stare at them.

I didn't want the experience coming between us. I wanted him to find a solution … which he did. Here is Bruce's story.

I AM AN OAK TREE

By Bruce Smith

I had a wonderful first weekend at the Hoffman family cottage with Colleen, her amazing sisters and family for a wonderful celebration of Phil and Sue's 50th wedding anniversary. I felt very moved and welcomed by the love and happiness that was shared with me and the special bond I felt with Colleen's triplet sisters.

After such a wonderful weekend, I felt rather shaken when Colleen spoke to me the following Monday night and told me each of her sisters liked me but were uncomfortable with my sexual energy, confirming Colleen's own concern experienced over the weekend.

I was grateful to Colleen for having raised the topic gently with me, having explained the issue in an open and caring way and having left me that night stating confidently that she knew I would find an answer. My home felt empty when she left as I knew I had nowhere to look but inward and I didn't like what I saw. I felt ashamed and disappointed in myself. I was afraid I had jeopardized my future with Colleen or lost the affection and respect of her sisters.

I woke early, lit a candle and went into meditation looking out my living room window at the beautiful beach and waters of Lake Ontario, obscured by an ancient oak tree that grew in my front yard. As I settled into myself and asked for my answer, I felt at peace and connected. I felt my legs extend into the cold dark soil below my home, grounding and connecting me to the power of the earth. My legs became roots intertwined with the mighty oak tree in the front yard and my body extended into the tree trunk. My arms reached for the heavens and multiplied into branches covered with lush healthy green foliage. I felt the sap running freely from my roots to the tips of my branches and realized that my life force was intermeshed with the energy of my beloved Colleen. That no woman but her could share that place of honor and life blood. I became aware of beautiful birds dancing in my branches seeking shelter from the storm and for comfort and nourishment from the seeds of the tree. I came to realize that the birds were Colleen's beautiful sisters and her girlfriends and many women who have flitted in and out of my life. Their dance in my branches was healthy and pleasant, but that none were entitled to share in my sexual energy. That special place was reserved for Colleen. I realized that would also create the safety for the healthy dance of the bird in my branches.

I then became aware of another strong oak tree standing beside me, rooted in the earth. That tree was my father and his life force was intertwined with my mother's and that many beautiful birds danced in his branches. Next to him were two other strong oak trees representing my brothers and their wives, along with networks of friends and loved ones.

I awakened gently with a deep understanding that I had found my answer. I then understood what it truly meant to love her sisters and girlfriends as a brother and to reserve my sexual energy solely for my beloved.

I told the story of the Oak Tree to Colleen and her sisters and felt a great healing. After that, all my female relationships improved and became healthier and more loving, in a great and safe way.

To this day, if I ever forget myself I smile and look into Colleen's eyes. I quietly say the words, "I am an oak tree."

When an attractive woman was around, like one of my gorgeous Goddess girlfriends, he would say to me under his breath, "I am an Oak Tree." It was his way of centering himself. If men and women could better understand this issue by gently speaking to and hearing each other, they would discover that the sacred beloved relationship is to honor each other and keep the relationship strong and comfortable.

My desire to respect myself and create a safe place allowed me to talk to Bruce and tell him what I didn't want in my life. My open and loving heart created the safeness for Bruce to find a solution. If jealousy is felt within a relationship, intimacy and trust can find a pathway together.

Case Study: ***Tom and Tracey***
Issues: **Lack of self-love, Jealousy**

Tom was first attracted by his wife Tracey's physical beauty. He loves the fact that she is attractive but he can't stand other men looking at her. Tom is possessive and controlling and his fear creates jealousy and misbehavior. Tracey has become fed up with his behavior and has shut down, making Tom even angrier.

Trust and open communication create a safe, loving connection between two people. Lack of self- love will trigger jealousy and jealousy can cause separation and dysfunctional behavior. Take responsibility if you are jealous or unsafe. Be independent and free to be all that you are with your beloved.

Keep your sexual energy for yourself and honor the people around you. Your sexual energy is part of your life force. Allow this energy to ignite you and be the reflection for others to find this ignition in themselves.

If you feel jealous or possessive, connect to this craving for love inside you. Go to the bridge and visualize the person you are jealous or possessive of, and explore your feelings, your void of self-love. Speak to them, expressing your fears and the need for their love.

Visualize this person who brings you to these uncomfortable emotions and see the emotional cord that attaches you to them. Cut it and re-connect with your own life force. Feel your open heart as you let go.

When I felt jealous when Bruce met my sisters, I went to my own feelings of self-doubt and lack of self-worth.

You Big Drip

If you are triggered by your partner and won't take responsibility for the truth within, you may experience a constant irritation that feels like a slow drip from a leaky faucet. This constant drip will slowly move into a place in you that has no tolerance. The drip will always draw you inside and make you uncomfortable until you release the emotions that are being stirred up – your own resentment and anger. Do the Inner Workout with this person, let go and re-connect. What is the relationship triggering in you? Open your heart and speak gently about how you feel.

Try not to blame or criticize the other person. Tell them how you feel when the irritation occurs. Take care of you and don't abandon the truth, share it without judgment and without the intention to hurt. Intimacy can be created. The dance of communication can be inspired with the open heart. If your partner shuts down or gets defensive, you don't have to take it personally. Don't abandon yourself. In that moment of truth, the drip may be the gift to share feelings. Your partner may not take care of the irritation. He may not honor the relationship enough, but you have a chance to put it on the table and share your feelings. This is part of taking care of you. Each person has a chance to show up, honor and respect another. Healthy communication about an issue can be an opportunity to love more.

When a drip on cement is constant, it will eventually erode the surface. Nagging becomes the drip when the issue is not taken care of. We won't get a positive response from someone if we nag, because the energy behind this communication is negative, and reminds the other person of their mother or father. They may react by shutting down or getting defensive and projecting because they feel like a bad boy/girl.

Women sometimes talk repeatedly about the same issue until everyone around them gets tired of hearing it. They become like the drip, constantly putting their husbands down. The energy of the experience creates resentment, shame, shut-down and blame.

Men and women dishonor their partners when they complain to their friends about the lack of sex in the relationship. Maybe the man or woman needs to look at why their partner is turned off …

It takes two to tango.

CHAPTER EIGHTEEN

Forgiveness

The Little Soul and The Sun

By Neale Donald Walsch

Neale Donald Walsch has written a wonderful children's book called *The Little Soul and The Sun*. I encourage anyone to read it. This beautiful story creates a pathway to forgiveness. I felt a huge weight lift from my shoulders when I realized that each soul that comes into our life and causes us pain has slowed down their vibration so that we can learn to forgive.

I was once in a relationship where I saw the soul pathways between myself and the other person. I realized in an instant that it was not possible for us to be together.

For me not to resent this person, I had to feel the pain and then let him go. As I forgave him my heart opened. He could not choose to be with me because he was here to live through his own personal darkness. This relationship opened up a door in me as I saw all of my past partners and how they each took me to my own depth of truth.

WE ATTRACT WHAT WE NEED, TO EXPERIENCE WHO WE ARE

My intensity in relationship is the search for truth and deeper learning. Once, when Bruce and I were on vacation, he expressed some issues. I had been feeling for some time that he was hiding or holding back some emotional wounds, parts of him that were shut down, or were in fear. When I questioned him he denied the concern. I betrayed myself and said that it was my self-worth that needed attention. Levels of truth shattered the wall of protection, and he admitted that he could not share his deep wound because he assumed that I couldn't handle it and he feared I would not love him.

This has happened to me in many relationships, where the man assumed that I didn't have the strength to go there and still love him if he showed me his darkness.

I felt betrayed initially, because Bruce was not able to share with me his truth and his fears. By Bruce facing his fear and working with it, I found a way to my open heart and we faced it together.

The Universe staged a perfect experience while we were on vacation. Bruce felt all of the parts of himself that he was hiding from me and from himself. He had assumed that I was fragile; he didn't know that I don't give up on love or truth when I am faced with despair, as long as I have time to feel and heal what comes up in me. He never felt safe in his previous relationships to show his vulnerability. Instead, he put on a strong front and faced it alone, never wanting to be perceived as weak.

Bruce faced some of his demons as I faced mine, and it took time and communication. Without judgment or blame, we carefully came back together. For my soul, this experience triggered my self-worth issues. I saw how I could stay connected while in relationship darkness.

All I ever wanted was to share my life with someone. If a man did not stay because he feared I would not love him, there was nothing I could do. It isn't about loving another, it's about me learning to love a deeper part of myself. Relationship brings me to aspects of me that yearn to be embraced, the parts that are ugly and the parts that are beautiful.

When I feel pain I welcome it because it is hooked onto my past. This is my journey to live more present. When I experience fear in another, I can make the choice not to own it, but if it comes up in me, it is mine. I was often afraid of the other person's darkness because they hid it from me. I was afraid of the pain I felt when I knew that they couldn't be in relationship with me and I felt them withdraw.

I know now that they had to leave the relationship so that they could be alone in another way, to find their own love that was in them. Forgiveness has shown me the pathway to love.

Once I went through this experience with Bruce, and he felt his own darkness and saw that I loved him more when he shared it with me, it was the beginning of a new level of belovedness. Bruce felt safe knowing that I would not judge him and I would not leave him. This was a part of a deepening of the emotions that moved our relationship to a deeper place.

Case Study: ***Helen, Robert, Arthur***
Issues: **Blame, Hurt, Resentment**

Helen and Robert are married and experiencing the beloved together. Helen is still heart-connected with a past relationship.

Helen's past relationship with Arthur keeps showing its face. Robert felt safe because Helen shared her truth as she moved through the past attachment triggered by Arthur.

Helen's safe relationship with Robert created the healing ground. She was truthful with Robert and talked about her heart connection with Arthur. When the opportunity arose and Helen saw why she could not have stayed with Arthur, she was finally able to detach completely.

Helen's hurt was that because Arthur didn't stay with her, she believed Arthur did not love her. She was attached to this aspect of the relationship, the part of her heart that believed he was responsible for the love she felt. When she realized that the love was always her love, she could let go of this hurt and the illusion that he had abandoned her, that the love wasn't real.

Robert's unfailing wisdom and understanding knew that if Helen healed that part of her heart she would be able to love more. Robert had the insight, self-acceptance and gentle love to hold the space for her. When she completely let go of Arthur, Robert felt the depth in her, which allowed him to go deeper within himself. Robert could then let go of any fear that she did not want to be with him. Helen let go of the hurt and the guilt, the abandoned love, and knew that it was her own love. She connected to the part of her heart she had shut down with Arthur when she forgave him. Robert could feel Helen's openness the moment he held her in his arms.

Each person in our lives is our soul's pathway to feel and evolve. Can we trust each other and try not to shut down our hearts? Love waits beyond the deep, dark pain. Move through it and allow the opening to heal your heart and allow your soul to live fully. Create the safe place in you and forgive.

CHAPTER NINETEEN

Need to be Right

The Ego Disguises Itself

by

Frannie Hoffman, author of

Modeling Clothes to Modeling Self:

A Journey of Remembering the Simple Truths of Love

The ego disguises itself as the knower.
Here is where I battle with my demon.
The heart embraces the wisdom.
The wisdom is in the space where sacred mystery lives.
Letting go of everything that I think I know,
allowing the knowledge to be.
It is right here now.
In the silent mind the truth is revealed.

Let me be still so that I can hear it's telling.
Let me be here now, in this moment, within my heart.
In the stillness the Spirit resurrects
and the love heals all.

— ❤ —

Sometimes our own control and need to be right can stop us from looking inside ourselves and seeing the truth. Our need to be right stops us from hearing another, as we try to convince someone that we know better or that our way is the answer.

When I judge someone for their behavior because it irritates me, I plug into them and want to make them wrong, creating a self-righteous experience. This behavior also creates separation in me. I try to use this experience to learn from it. My ego may keep me connected to a part in another that I don't like in myself. My mother was always busy and she always got things done. Instead of judging her or telling her that she should do something differently, I chose to see the same thing in myself and to see it as a positive not a negative. My mother taught me how to accomplish my goals, to take action. When I was a child she was busy all the time and I couldn't feel her loving herself. I thought her days were a struggle but I see it differently now. Getting things done gave her the love. I try to feel my love while I'm busy and when it's tiresome or hard, I try to feel that too. When I'm busy, it's hard to be present with my relationships, but connecting to myself and being present with someone at the same time can be a good balance.

My father worried about what other people thought. Instead of staying in my ego and judging my father, I am grateful to know that I can stop worrying about others or taking care of everyone else and take the time to take care of myself. Eventually the experience allowed me to move into a different place so that I didn't leave myself. I used the bridge to disconnect from past relationships of pain or the judgment of ego so that I could be the knower of truth. I used this experience to find the pathway to my own heart and self-knowledge.

Rejection

Rejection can be devastating and may stop the trust and openness with someone, eventually blocking intimacy. If we have been rejected, our abandonment wound can bring us to our own void of love. Rejection can be healed even when we aren't in an intimate relationship.

If we reject another person's opinion, if we reject someone's open heart, if we reject someone's voice of truth, that person will eventually withdraw. Rejection hurts and stops the flow of safeness and love in the relationship. Practice on the bridge by using these relationships to feel the rejection and hurt. Detach from these people and re-connect to your own safe love. If someone shuts down, they are rejecting their own open heart, and rejecting their own love. Take back your power and find your own way out of rejection. Heal your own rejected heart and fill your void with self-awareness. You will then be attractive and can attract the relationship that will not reject you.

Respect

We sometimes cannot see the grandness of love because we are stuck in our own human doubt and fear. It's up to us to take care of this doubt and know that love and the beloved are experienced more fully as we release into all that we are. Keep the beloved relationship alive in partnership. It is our job and purpose to find our way to our highest vibration in all aspects of our life. To live in this vibration is to remember who the other person is with respect. If they cannot live in this place with you, it's time for you to recognize it and respect yourself enough to leave.

Case Study: *Veronica*
Issues: **Self-respect**

Veronica was in a relationship with Nick for almost six years. She was having anxiety attacks, feeling very disrespected by Nick. As she began to unfold the truth, she realized that Nick's anger and need to be right created a shift in her comfortableness with him. Veronica was shutting down with Nick and his judgment and criticism made her feel she wasn't good enough. Veronica started to become inauthentic, saying and doing things for Nick's love and approval.

Nick was still married and living with his wife and children in another city. He had health and financial issues that kept him stuck and unavailable. Veronica continued to wait for Nick but he was always making excuses about why he couldn't leave his life and be with her. Nick's wife knew about Veronica and accepted the way things were.

The first question I asked Veronica was, "Why do you accept this kind of relationship for yourself?" We started the process of self-discovery and Veronica opened her heart to truth, her lack of self-acknowledgement and her fears.

Why did Veronica accept empty promises and become unavailable to herself? Why did Veronica disrespect herself by allowing Nick to judge and criticize her? Why did Veronica disrespect Nick's wife by staying in the relationship?

The *Pocket Guide to your He♥rt* process helped Veronica with her inner safeness. She took Nick onto the bridge and used him to find the strength and feel her self-worth. The Inner Workout helped Veronica to feel her:

- fear of not being loved
- fear of being alone
- void of love
- unworthiness and self-worth issues
- disrespect and judgment of herself
- guilt and disrespect

Veronica let go of the perception that Nick was responsible for her love or her pain. Her self-awareness listened to her heart and she saw that each hurtful experience with Nick served her to feel and heal her past.

Veronica started to speak up with Nick when she felt that he was disrespecting her. By facing her fear, she finally had the courage to write him a letter.

If you are in a relationship that does not feel comfortable, this letter may inspire you to write your own letter of truth without blame or judgement.

Dear Nick,

I can't change your perception of how things are. Nor do I want to. You see things as you do for whatever reason. I can only explain things from my perspective. And this is what I've tried to do.

I have tried to discuss certain obstacles with you but there has never been any resolution of them.

I guess in all the work I've done, in all the clearing out of past pain, I see clearly where I am today and the behavior of those around me from a place of truth. I take responsibility for my own emotions and I take care of them in a healthy way.

You did not have to struggle alone. All you had to do was ask for help. From me, from Julie, from a therapist, whomever you felt comfortable with. It was your choice to struggle alone. It was my choice to seek the help I needed and wanted. And my healthy choices were supported.

I don't want to put myself in the line of fire anymore. I really want someone who is willing to face their own truths instead of blaming others for their failings. Someone who can take ownership of their behavior and misbehavior and not blame others. I must deal with my own issues.

You are a writer. Words are the tools you use to try to weave your magic. But I am no longer under your spell.

If you seek understanding or clarification, if you want to know why things turned out as they did, perhaps you might go inside yourself and look for some answers.

I have explained my feelings time and again. You choose not to believe me. I think it's clear there is no need to go on with this.

Veronica

Veronica and Nick are not in relationship any longer. She finally had to let go and say that she wanted more. Veronica's self-respect has protected her heart. She continues to evolve and take care of herself.

Thank you Veronica for sharing your intimate words.

Isolation/Shut Down

When someone shuts down or runs, abandoning love, he/she is experienced as being the isolator. He/she can't get too close for fear of being absorbed. Usually the person who feels this way was smothered by one of his/her parents and hated it. So if anyone comes into their life with love and attention, especially if it's needy, they run from it. Feeling the uncomfortableness with this kind of energy would be, for a man, like his mother, or for a woman, like her father experience.

Outside Elements

There are outer elements that affect our hearts: shut-down, cold hearts or the projection of anger that is hot and driven by the wind of toxic resentment. We have to take time and move into our inner connection to self, so that we can keep the fire – our inner thermostat – alive. We need to:

- Keep our body comfortable by taking steps to take care of ourselves for protection, strength and nourishment.
- Clothe ourselves so that we're protected and not vulnerable.

- Practice self-knowledge and build a strong self-worth, so that our heart can be safe and open.
- Allow the experience of the outer cold elements to witness our safe emotional state.
- Keep our inner furnace on high, to handle the outer discomforts. It may get colder with storms that will test us but we will feel the calm wisdom that follows.
- Prepare ourselves so that we will be open to change.
- Take care of our fear and support ourselves so that we can feel the safeness in us.
- Let go of other people's fear or connection to illusion.
- Allow reality to move us into our own comfort within so that it doesn't matter what the elements are, we can still be comfortable … feeling good in our skin.

When we are present and aware of what is happening we can connect with our quiet peace within while the roaring winds and turbulent energies surround us. We can be the peaceful observer looking out of our safe living room while the snow or rain dances on the other side of the window.

Be Available

Any acts of misbehavior are for our soul's evolution and the opportunity to be available for ourselves. It's not about being anything for anyone. It's about being there for ourselves. If we're available for ourselves we'll attract someone who is going to show up and be available for themselves and for us. Our own availability can keep us present, satisfied and healthy.

CHAPTER TWENTY

Authenticity

All that is real and authentic cannot be destroyed.

I saw the past dances of love and pain and I became grateful instead of resentful. Bruce says that is what he was attracted to, my soft open energy and gentleness. I saw the same reflection in him. It was comfortable!

When issues in either Bruce or myself surface, we see this as an opportunity to love more. Our healing process begins when we recognize the other person is shut down or feeling uneasy.

For example:

If Bruce comes home feeling shut down from a day of hell on Bay Street, I hold a safe place for him to feel what he needs to process or take care of himself. That may mean talking about it with me or taking a sauna and spending time with himself.

The truth is, we feel the other person's uncomfortableness right away. Why pretend?

Intimacy is sharing, but it doesn't mean we have to dump or project on the other person.

Honor each other by creating a safe place and hold this space for them if they are closed.

Don't allow anyone to disrespect you by taking their bad day out on you!!

Usually, just expressing to me that he had a bad day is all Bruce needs to do to unlock the tension and emotional weight he's carrying.

We can't fix anyone but sometimes we need to let them feel their lack of love or self-doubt. Sometimes we just have to be with the pain for a while.

During this time, connect to yourself as you breathe into your own openness.

Be the reflection of faith and hope.

If you become shut down when your partner is shut down, your reflection keeps you stuck, unhappy and communication stops for a while.

Truth

Sometimes we may know the truth of our own plan and we hold back this truth because we believe we are protecting our partner. If we speak honestly, they may need to go to their pain or void so that they can heal. We then give them the opportunity to make their own choice instead of trying to protect them. Let go of control.

When we are living in open heart and loving unconditionally, our heart places a hand of truth over the other person's heart, reflecting faith in the places where there is self-doubt and despair. This is where we can hold the space when the other person is in pain and is going through their darkness. It's like an unspoken truth to remind us, to remind each other, when we forget. This trust and loyalty is a commitment to each other, and the safe bond of understanding is stronger than any piece of paper or certificate.

Try to hold the space while the other person finds their own open heart. If you can remember the love, instead of hooking in or engaging, the need to seek past pain and to let go of it can move both of you through the experience.

The result will be to feel more love within and with each other. I changed my dance step in relationship and each experience deepens me and the love that I have to give.

Safe Ground

Our immediate reaction or instinct may be to say no ... to be right. Listen to the other person and let go of control. Be open to hear what they have to say because we all have an opinion. This can be the opening of more safeness instead of more shut down.

We may think we know better and we may have experienced something that we feel strongly about. If we are not open to listen, we may not know if someone else's experience can direct us to a better place. In partnership, the other person may need something in the moment. If we don't hear them because we're not open to another, we may miss important information. Can we give the other person the benefit of the doubt, and allow the experience to unfold so that we can both be heard and respected, instead of one person controlling it and taking action? Together, in that moment, there can be a choice. We can look at both sides. It's important to look after ourselves, but sometimes we realize we have to give a little bit more. When we give, it's important that there be no resentment attached. Make sure that your heart is satisfied and feels good.

I Can't Get No Satisfaction

Song title, The Rolling Stones

Some people feel they can't get any satisfaction because they're waiting for someone else to satisfy them. I believe that it's up to us to satisfy ourselves and then we won't be disappointed. With our own needs of passion, intimacy and sexuality, satisfaction comes from the inner contentment of an open heart, of self-acceptance with our gentle mind.

Two willing people, ignited in their own love can experience the dance of past pain and the dance of present joy together.

To show up to Dance is the greatest Beloved Relationship you can experience

CAN WE STAY IN LOVE WHEN OUR PARTNER FORGETS THEIR OWN LOVE OR WORTH? TURN ON, DON'T TURN OFF

If the man is the controller and sets rules that introduce fear, it will only encourage shut-down in the relationship. His partner's fear, lack of self-love and self-worth will be unattractive. Fear-based control can be a turn-off and causes separation between two people. If a woman is angry all the time or constantly disappointed, self-righteous or aggressive, her uncomfortable behavior will turn the man off. Some men try to make things comfortable, by giving or becoming the good boy, trying to make "mommy" happy. Both partners become inauthentic and unattractive to one another. Control, fear or anger creates an unsafeness that stops the desire of love with another.

You Don't Know Until You Know!

As I've said before, you don't know until you know. You can't share safe love unless you have experienced it. You cannot live it if you haven't known it. In the movie *City of Angels*, Meg Ryan's boyfriend doesn't understand intimacy and how to communicate feelings. He only knows what he knows and is unaware of the experience of deep feelings of love that Meg Ryan begins to experience with the angel (Nicolas Cage). Nicolas Cage's character lives in the passion of the open, beloved heart and Meg Ryan is ignited as she feels those aspects in herself. She wants this kind of experience with her boyfriend, but he doesn't know how to give it, share it or be in it. So when Meg Ryan's boyfriend decides that it's time to propose, he barges into the locker room and blurts it out: "Let's hop on a plane and go to Tahoe and get married. You know you're made for me. Let's get together. It's perfect, so why wait … let's do it now." For some people that kind of proposal is fine, but in the movie, it represents the depth of the character's personal connection to love and intimacy – he didn't know any other way. Meg Ryan knew he wasn't ignited in the way Nicolas Cage was and she didn't feel the spark that she knew was in herself. She had got a glimpse of what she wanted and how she could feel deeply within while experiencing the energy of the angel (Nicolas Cage). She knew what she was missing with her boyfriend because she felt the difference. ***You don't know until you know!***

No Attachments

When we are attached to a thought, person or picture of what we think we want, there isn't room for a better opportunity. Can we let go of attachments of what we feel is best for us or another? God's plan is better than ours.

If we can feel good with nothing, we can attract everything ... the possibilities are endless. Let go of your picture!

Struggle happens when we try to control, hold onto or force our attached beliefs. Find the space within, beyond the pain, and allow your life to show you the plan.

Life is all about Letting Go

What's Mine Is Yours ...

In the beloved relationship, there isn't any "*this is mine and this is yours.*" To change that to "*what's mine is yours*" is a healthier communication and experience. We can witness this in the issue of control with money. I have lived this in the past and have observed it in many relationships. The husband is the breadwinner and the wife doesn't have her own money. She's constantly having to ask her husband for money. It gives the impression that he doesn't value what his wife does – taking care of the home, the children and him, while creating a beautiful place to live. A woman who creates the peaceful, loving energy within expresses herself through her family. It's always important that each partner be valued and appreciated. It goes both ways. The homemaker must not devalue her partner and her husband must honor and respect her.

Case Study: *Elsa and Peter*
Issues: **Bully/Victim**

Elsa left her career to be with her children, but she didn't take care of her anger and suppressed emotions. She blames her husband for her unhappiness. Peter is working in a very high-pressure job and has to come home after a full day and take care of Elsa and the children. The truth is that Peter doesn't want to come home. He's exhausted and all he wants is to feel safe and comfortable in his home environment. The tension is always high and Elsa projects anger while Peter walks on eggshells. Peter just wants peace and supports her with anything she needs to help her be comfortable. However, Elsa doesn't seem to value him and only thinks about how much more help he can give her, and it's never enough.

We're all capable of respecting or disrespecting our partner. We have to work on respecting ourselves instead of blaming another.

Any kind of misbehavior is linked to lack of love within the person or the relationship. Find that place inside that feels resentment or blame and take responsibility for it. Appreciate who you are, what you have attracted and take care of finding the truth.

LIVE GRATEFULLY AND LIVE GREAT.

Walking On Eggshells

Everyone understands the phrase "walking on eggshells." As a child and teenager, I remember experiencing this because I wanted to be a good girl for love. At times I watched what I said or did in order not to feel disappointment or disapproval.

I behaved this way in relationships because sometimes I got caught off-guard and scolded, projected onto or shut out by someone. I would find myself walking on eggshells.

Why was I in fear?
How did I stop myself from being my natural self?
I wanted to be loved so badly that
I would be CAREFUL.

This pattern is a result of personal experience and choice. We are the ones who choose to watch what we say or do ... including walking on eggshells around someone.

Now that I'm aware of this experience I try to tune into what I'm feeling in the moment. So do I:

- Give my power to them and shut down?
- React and become angry?
- Try to make the person comfortable?
- Feel fear?
- Find my own connection and plug into me and feel what I need to feel?
- Feel my lack or disappointment?
- Open my heart to me and find my center?

Solutions I can then decide on:

- If I'm not safe to talk about it, then I'll withdraw.
- If I feel safe to talk, I'll tell them how I feel.
- If I realize that my relationship with someone is like walking on eggshells, I'll use this person and take them onto the bridge. I'll talk about it there as I visualize the experience with them. I'll find my way back to my inner strength and self-worth. I continue to practice so I won't need this experience in my life any longer.

I can now see that my own children and my other relationships sometimes find themselves in the position of walking on eggshells, especially if I'm shut down or tentative. We're all capable of making that choice ... to walk carefully with the attachment of doing or saying the right thing for love and approval.

Move past the fear with someone and talk about your uncomfortableness with them on the bridge. Either way, you have to feel your fears and lack. That's what this behavior pattern is telling you. Take responsibility and use the experience to shift you.

Be all that you are.

**WALKING ON EGGSHELLS
IS OUR CHOICE
STAYING THERE
IS ALSO OUR CHOICE**

CHAPTER TWENTY-ONE

Infidelity

What is Infidelity?

Infidelity: Marital unfaithfulness, an act of adultery.
Running from your matrimonial bed
into the arms of another.

Infidelity may be a desperate choice when needs are not met and if couples are not communicating. If the husband feels that he is never good enough and the wife doesn't feel her own love, she may be shut down. If neither is filling the other up – they look for another love to fill the void. Create a safe place and open heart (without blame or judgment). Talk before you hide or run. Honor your partner and respect them enough to be truthful. Infidelity can become a barrier to trust and is not an appropriate band-aid.

Case Study: *Kathy*
Issues: **Infidelity, Self-worth, Shame Victim, Anger, Resentment**

Kathy came to me in tears. Her husband was having an affair and she was devastated, feeling anger, blame and humiliation. Kathy was feeling her "victim" and her self-worth was very low. She didn't want to be angry toward her husband for fear he would leave, so she projected it on the other woman. Kathy spent time with me, feeling her discomfort, and I showed her how to go inside and face both her husband and his mistress. She confessed to the pain, judgment, resentment, anger, fear and sadness and Kathy felt emotions that had been suppressed for years. She realized that she and her husband had not created time for each other. Kathy was so busy with her career and being a mom, she put her husband on the back burner, ignoring the relationship. She saw that the intimacy and love was not nurtured. Kathy was always busy and preoccupied by the future instead of being present with her partner.

Kathy forgave her husband because she didn't want to lose the relationship. She felt her Goddess self very powerful and so did he. Kathy took 50% of the responsibility and her husband stopped seeing the other woman. It was very important that Kathy let go of blame and resentment, because if she couldn't, her husband would continue to feel the shut-down or inauthentic behavior that triggered his guilty boy.

If there is infidelity in a relationship, guilt will trigger shame and this dance will become tiresome and uncomfortable. The only way the relationship can overcome an affair is if the other person can truly let go – becoming safe within the relationship is the challenge. The heart shuts down and the other person can feel it immediately, triggering guilt or blame. If the person who had the affair becomes distant or unpresent, the other person will assume the worst. Once the safeness is gone, it's hard to shift into peace and love with the partner.

Kathy took ownership of her past and the breakdown of the relationship. Did her husband let go of his guilt and take ownership of the betrayal? That is an important step and presents a great opportunity for healing.

There are so many issues woven into an experience like this. If you can take 50% of the responsibility – each of you has the opportunity to heal. You then have a choice to grow and become the beloved. Forgiveness is a major player. Forgive the other and yourself.

Infidelity usually destroys a partnership, leaving deep, unresolved issues. Betrayal triggers issues of trust, self-worth and neediness, shame, guilt and resentment that can shut down the heart and cause separation. All behaviors can result in inauthenticity. If each person can take responsibility and forgive, there can be an opportunity for growth, more love and intimacy and a second chance to do it differently, creating a more authentic relationship. Take each other onto the bridge and feel! Let go! Even if you end up leaving the relationship, one day you will let go ... why not do it now?

LET GO!

Self-hatred can ignite the fire or craving in an unavailable relationship.

When I go into the zone that is hooked onto a past relationship, I can see that the craving was triggered by the person who couldn't stay connected in the relationship and became unavailable.

The fire was ignited deep within both of us because I was not available to myself and he was not available to me or to himself. The fire created need and, for me, was the experience of wanting Daddy's love. For him, the love was the fix, the comfort of being ignited and loved by me.

I have learned a truth about this unavailable male type who is good with words and wooing because he may be addicted to something – self-hatred or self-destruction (it could be an addiction to love, drinking, smoking, medication or drugs) – that keeps him distracted and unavailable to himself. Another truth is that we may all be addicted to something. Being a workaholic is another way of being unavailable.

When we look at our own addiction to love and see clearly how our neediness allows the experience of unavailability, disregard or abandonment, we can feel the part of us that has denied our own truth and self-love. Self-hatred brews in this place where we disconnect from ourselves, giving the power to someone else.

Detach from the thought that this is the one or ever could have been the one, because this particular truth sits beyond the excuses; the forgiveness and the illusion. I used my anger and truth to detach from the illusion and once I let go of him, I saw the reality.

He was unavailable and couldn't be there for me.

Inner Relationship – *Create a safe place.*

Inner Workout – *Use these past or present relationships to feel all of your own self-hatred.*

Inner Peace – *Re-connect to your own fire and live fully with another in safe love.*

CHAPTER TWENTY-TWO

Show Up—Stay Connected

Judgment, or an image of what you think it should look like, might stop the relationship from deepening. When two people come together, the process of self-discovery and getting to know each other work hand in hand. Physical expectations may stop us from getting to know someone. Self-awareness or self-acceptance may not have been experienced yet.

When Bruce and I met, I experienced relationship totally differently. The places in me that were closed or unsafe because of past experiences slowly shifted as I opened to the opportunity of getting to know him. At first I closed sexually because I didn't feel the spark. Instead of blaming him or making him responsible, I used this safe relationship to create the spark in myself. Once I felt completely safe, the opening exploded into the passion between us.

Our relationship deepens as we each find new depths in ourselves, holding the space for one another when issues come up. I realize that I never knew how much love I could feel until I was safe to experience the darkness in me, allowing for more love once I let go.

While I healed my past with Bruce, he held the space for me by not shutting down.

The key is, we showed up, we didn't run, hide or blame. We spoke truth, lived with our feelings and honored each other. We continue to live together with this formula to help us grow emotionally and spiritually. Show up for yourself and with each other. Feel, communicate and hold a safe space. Let go of past pain, find new love and constantly spark the relationship.

Some women don't see that their men show up. They are caught up in their own uncomfortableness or shut down by distractions. When their partner comes home, their own moodiness or victim energy can create the separation and the partner may feel like he isn't good enough or feels unsafe to talk about it. Eventually the man will shut down and leave emotionally. Shut-down in one can create shut-down in the other. This is a great opportunity to take responsibility for our issues and find a way to stop the blame and judgment. Many of our parents stayed in disconnected relationships. Our generation has many broken homes because one or both partners end the relationship to stop the pain of reliving, over and over, the mother/father dance.

CAN WE SHOW UP TO HEAL?

When a woman feels her own connection to self-worth and realizes that her source of love is in her, she can find that safe place to communicate the truth, whether or not her partner is open. This connection with her heart can find a way to talk about issues, struggles or feeling unappreciated. If she has taken care of her resentment, she can communicate without blame or judgment, creating a safe place to take care of herself, while listening to what her partner may have to say.

If the man takes care of his resentment or disappointments and finds his way to his open heart, he can create the supportive place with his arms and heart for her to share her feelings. This humble and vulnerable place creates safeness and can encourage healthy communication without blame or judgment.

Case Study: ***Paul and Joan***
Issue: Communication, Are You Listening?

When Paul and Joan drove past a flea market and Paul wanted to stop, Joan said, "Let's not." He got mad at her and Joan reached into her heart and said, "You can have all the junk you want, it's just that it's leaking into my space. Can you sort it out before you buy more?" He agreed and they both felt good about it.

If we can find our own way to our open heart and speak from this place (without blame, disappointment, resentment or anger), we can communicate from our fullness – not from our void. We can then say what we're truly feeling so that there is room in the conversation for compromise instead of control. Allow each person the space to feel and speak from truth.

When we can listen to one another, the healing can be in the silence between the emotions. The experience becomes one of lifting up the emotion to be felt. Synchronicity is the mystery that will guide the dance between two people. It is easier to go with it and allow the emotion to have a voice by taking ownership of the truth that waits to be embraced. It takes one person staying centered to remind another. It takes two people to show up and weave with one another.

TALK TO EACH OTHER AND LISTEN TO ONE ANOTHER!
DON'T SHUT DOWN
IF YOU HAVE SOMETHING
TO TALK ABOUT
SHARE IT!
IF YOU ARE IN A RELATIONSHIP
WHERE YOU HAVE GIVEN IT YOUR ALL
AND NOTHING HAS SHIFTED
STAND UP AND SAY ...
THIS IS NOT GOOD ENOUGH FOR ME!

Breaking Up Is Hard To Do

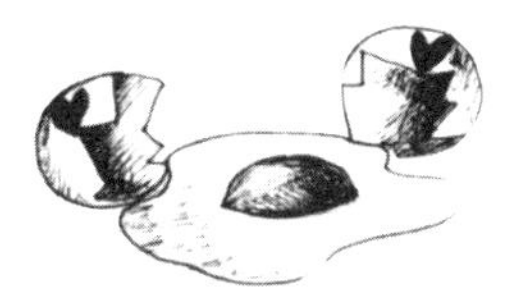

I just talked with Grace, who can't deal with her boyfriend's rudeness any longer. She wants to break up with him. As she tells me about how he treats her, the anger and resentment pours out. I asked if she had ever communicated these uncomfortable experiences with him and she reported that she had always shut down and pretended that everything was okay.

Grace visualized the bridge and created a safe place where she confronted her boyfriend, who had behaved exactly like all of her past relationships. The Inner Workout opened her to what she was feeling. On the Bridge ...

GRACE SHOUTED AT HIM
SHE TOLD HIM HOW SHE FELT
HER HEART FELT THE HURT
SHE FELT UNLOVED BY HIM
HIS CRITICISM AND DISREGARD MADE HER FEEL JUDGED
GRACE FELT HER VOID WITH HIM

Grace saw the emotional cord connected to her boyfriend. She cut the cord and immediately re-connected to her life force. Grace saw how she had believed him and given away her power. She felt her compassionate, open heart as she forgave him for not knowing how to love. She realized he loved her the only way he knew how.

Grace felt her own self-acceptance and didn't need his love or approval any longer. She stood in front of him on the bridge and connected to her strength and beautiful heart. Grace saw that she denied her own love in any relationship and realized that, for her, they all represented the experience of not standing up to her father, who controlled her for love and approval.

A few days later, Grace felt empowered as she ended the relationship with her boyfriend. She was firm as she told him that he wasn't what she desired or needed in a relationship. Grace thanked him for showing her how she stopped loving herself by putting up with his dishonoring behavior. She could speak to him without blame and she shared with him what the relationship had shown her. Grace's heart was open and he felt safe as he heard what she said. They both saw how they had contributed to the break-up and because Grace was not in anger, he didn't shut down.

Breaking up can be the opportunity for healing.

Betrayal or rejection can embrace our lack of self-worth. Years later we can experience a new level of healing when the experience shows its face again. We have an opportunity to be truthful as the betrayal or rejection moves into the experience.

We don't have to attract the same experience over and over again if we use it to feel our own issues.

Self-Hatred / Anger / Punishment / Disrespect

We may use the experiences of punishment, judgment and blame to find our way back from feeling self-hatred to self-love. Suppressed self-hatred can be experienced as self-righteousness or anger. Projecting onto another can feed the ego. Scolding, judging or criticizing someone else to diminish them is a dishonoring behavior that hurts and shuts down any relationship. Take a look at how you treat loved ones or friends and discover the truth in your communication and body language.

**WHERE DO YOU DESIRE TO BE ...
IN LOVE OR IN HATE?**

He Didn't Choose Me

I have had a relationship where someone did not choose me and it took me a long time to release the attachment of not being loved by this person. I felt the hurt and betrayal of not being the chosen one. I realized that the love I felt with this person was not the love that he gave me, it was the love I felt, which was mine all along. I came to understand this while I was in a relationship with another person and was able to release it. I could then detach from him and open my heart fully to love more. Finally, I knew that it wasn't about needing anyone's love or having anyone love me to feel good. I realized that the love was mine all along. I AM THE LOVE. Every relationship in which I have been abandoned, betrayed or needy had one thing in common – they were all a form of love. I stood back and saw that all the issues, all the patterns with all of the pain and misbehaviors, were created to redirect my connection to love. It all melted into the union of myself as I realized that every relationship showed me a different level of the love I had in me. If they didn't choose me, if they didn't show up or they weren't there, I knew that the love was still there because the love was my own.

If we choose to stay attached to the void, the neediness, the yearning and the pain, then we are not feeling our own gentle love. Don't be a victim.

**EACH RELATIONSHIP SHOWS US
DIFFERENT LEVELS OF OUR OWN LOVE
IT IS NOT THEIR LOVE
IT IS OUR LOVE THAT WE FEEL.**

**EACH RELATIONSHIP IS THE OPPORTUNITY
TO LOVE MORE
OR LOVE LESS**

Meditation*...Letting go of the person you are waiting for...the one who isn't showing up...the one who has abandoned you.*

Breathe... connect to your energy and visualize your bridge. Take this person onto the bridge – the one you're waiting for, the one you're feeling not good enough with, the one that is withholding and withdrawing or shutting down. Speak to them and share the truth of how you feel. Let the uncomfortable feelings have a voice inside you and allow them to move through you as you go through the process of confronting this person with your suppressed emotions. As you feel them, release the truth – by crying or just feeling the anxiety of it. As you speak the words, you will anchor the emotions and release them all at the same time. Feel the emotions in you as you look at this person, the one who is affecting you and making you crazy with fear, emptiness or yearning. Use him or her and tell them about how you feel with them. They are the gift to help you go there and feel. See the attachment to them with a cord running between you…count to three…cut the cord or chop it, disconnect it in some way, and then breathe into your own source of love and allow the energy of your own love and respect to be felt. Breathe and connect with your energy from the root (base of your spine), move it up through your body and open your heart as you forgive him/her and let them go. This is emotionally disconnecting. You can then say, "I don't need your love. I don't need your approval. I don't need you to open to me. I forgive you. My heart is open. I can feel my own love. This is MY love, not your love. THIS IS MY LOVE. I let you go." (It doesn't mean you're letting go of the relationship or that you won't see the person, but you're letting go of feeling that they're the one who is responsible for your love or approval.) Feel your source of power and self-acceptance.

You can look back on all your relationships and see that they have been a form of needy love or abandoned love, a love that creates the yearning because you feel the void, the emptiness, the loss, the disappointment. Show up for yourself and know that one of these relationships, one of these experiences can help you heal. You don't have to go back to each one, but if you still feel the relationship is triggering you and you feel the person is affecting your heart, take them to the bridge. If they trigger you when you think of them or hear their voice, put them on the bridge. If you see them and you feel closed or uncomfortable, then you'll know there is still an attachment, that issues are still living in you and you are not finished with them, even if they are long gone. You don't have to be with this person to resolve it. The confrontation is on the bridge, inside you. If it isn't an intimate relationship, if they have moved away and you may never see them again, you can still take them onto the bridge.

We are all energy and remembering someone can take us right to the emotions or the experience to feel, as if they were in front of us. Use them to feel the emotions that the relationship has brought up for you and then create an opportunity to open the part of your heart that has been closed by this experience or person. Realize that the love is yours and open your own heart as you release the hurt, pain and resentment that is in your body and stops you from loving fully.

CHAPTER TWENTY-THREE

Three Aspects of Relationship

Disrespect – Respect – Self-Respect

"Enjoyment, passion and fun keep love alive.
Duty, obligation and lack of
communication poison the relationship."
The Incidental Guru by Cindy Stone

Relationships have provided my greatest experiences to get to know more of myself. We cannot discount the relationships that have been a struggle. This is where we can learn the most about our dark side. Usually the hard relationship mirrors for us the places inside where we don't feel the love or where we deny ourselves love. We can take care of the issue for ourselves and come to understand that we don't need the unloving lesson any longer. When the relationship experience feels like a duty or is unsafe or uncomfortable, the love can slowly die. Say, "YES! With every cell of my body I believe!"

The freedom of enjoyment, passion and fun, healthy intimacy, trust and safe love keeps love and relationships healthy and alive!

I have always known that respect is a major player in a healthy relationship. Respecting others has been important to me but respecting myself has been missing at times.

I have been disrespected in some close relationships when the other person has used words – mean words of judgment and blame – to scold me or disempower me. They would not take ownership of their projection, and I was unable to convince them. They had their own truth and believed themselves. The worst thing I could do was not respect myself.

I have come to realize and accept that you can leave a relationship when you feel there is lack of respect. Another healthy way to look at it is *you leave a relationship to respect yourself*. This choice creates the experience of taking back your power as you take responsibility for the issue and the uncomfortable relationship.

In the past, I kept losing respect for myself when I repeatedly went back to a relationship after a hurtful experience to love again, unconditionally. This place within me gave away my power, bit by bit. Being scolded, demeaned or judged by anyone is disrespectful. But there are limits and boundaries crossed when someone wants to disempower you. Your safeness and comfort levels are fragile.

When I have crossed that boundary, I do everything I can to apologize. I never set out to hurt anyone, so when I can make amends and create a safe place for healing, I know that I have opened another part of myself.

Human nature is made up mostly of imperfections. I look forward to continuing to learn about myself, with all the ups and downs. The way I choose to learn and grow in relationship includes taking responsibility for my own anger, my inauthenticity and my self-respect.

Working relationships can create disrespect. The people we work with may not treat us or others with respect. We may find the courage to speak calmly and firmly to the person when they project self-righteousness and treat us badly, but how many times can we do it? Projecting back in anger or disrespect or shutting down isn't appropriate either. When the pattern recurs, we don't feel safe to be our natural self.

Look at the way you breathe or how uncomfortable you really are. If the other person is in a good mood and everything is running smoothly, you might start feeling a little more comfortable and safe, but suddenly the old pattern returns. Maybe the projection is onto another person, yet it is openly experienced by everyone around. Feel the energy among the group; feel the tentativeness hanging around.

Those that do not take ownership for their suppressed issues, angers, resentments and unsettled emotions have uptight energy moving within them. This experience can cause behaviors and reactions that include both flare-ups and shut-downs. All parties feel inauthentic, unproductive and less creative or open. The inauthenticity comes from the one who is projecting or not respecting others and is experienced by the ones not respecting themselves.

Respecting yourself gives great comfort and makes the gift of respecting another more loving. When I understood this deep within myself, it was like I had taken a needle and thread and put in a few stitches to mend the tender wound of past and present, my lack of self-worth and self-love. This personal respect empowered me and helped me heal and let go of relationships I had been hurt by – great gifts to bring me to self-respect.

People may treat us inappropriately and when there isn't a safeness we don't have to try to prove anyone wrong, and we don't need their approval – there is really no debate – we must try to take gentle care of our self.

When people come to you in open heart you can feel the safeness. The opening is there, in the experience of self-love and respect.

When I surrendered myself to preserve the relationship or walked on eggshells in order to create an inauthentic safeness, I became inauthentic. I harmed my self-worth. I was stifled and couldn't find my light. I relinquished my self-respect and the other person crossed my boundaries.

To stay in a relationship that is unsafe, where you cannot breathe fully, is your choice. Respect yourself enough to say no, I am now in a different place. To breathe fully in every relationship means taking care of your own self-love and self-respect.

Be the light – always be true to yourself – RESPECT

If you are in relationship with someone who is disrespectful you must define your limits. When they cross the boundaries you must take care of yourself. You must withdraw. Try not to disrespect yourself or compromise yourself to appease someone. It can disempower you. Self-respect will empower you.

The process of letting go of your disrespectful relationship brings up feelings of self-doubt, grief, guilt, pain and suffering. My *Pocket Guide to your He♥rt* formula supports the process of letting go of the uncomfortable emotions and issues that overwhelm the heart.

Take responsibility and take back your power. When you find your way back to your compassionate heart without blame, forgive yourself and the other person. You can then say in truth, "I love you and I can let you go."

I have personally experienced relationships where my voice was not respected and I stopped speaking. That was my way of protecting myself, and it stopped my personal growth and shut down my spirit. Self-protection and silence may be a safe place for a while, but only until you find the courage to move into a more truthful experience. Self-respect can free your spirit!

CHAPTER TWENTY-FOUR

Female and Male Energy

We are all energy and we can experience ourselves and others by being aware of both the feminine and masculine energy. From the girly girl topped up with female energy to the macho guy solid with male energy. The lack of energy or abundance of it can protect or hide a multitude of issues. This energy can also give away the secrets we try to hide.

My female energy was very high and my naïve nature and needy heart attracted major disappointment and loss. I was very feminine and my soft side led me to places where I was easily manipulated or controlled. As I experienced some hard times, my masculine energy moved more into balance, allowing me the courage, strength and fortitude to make healthier choices.

Although I feel a lot more balanced, some days I find myself experiencing more of my feminine than my masculine energy and other days my male energy needs to take action or stand up for myself. This balance in me creates a more attractive, centered persona.

For a woman, the balance of female/male energy is the union within, creating the Goddess. I have witnessed this unfolding with most of my female clients who commit to the relationship within and deal with their own issues of fear, abandonment, past pain or resentment. **THE GODDESS ... THE BALANCE ... VERY ATTRACTIVE ... VERY EXCITING ... EASY TO BE WITH.**

A macho man who creates a rough and tough shell may have no desire to connect to his emotions or soft, sensitive heart. His masculine energy protects him from his feelings. He doesn't know any other way. Often this shell is shattered because of tough lessons or traumatic loss. Once shaken up, his feminine, sensitive nature humbles him and takes him to a very vulnerable place. As his female energy strengthens, his intimacy and relationships can usually become more balanced. For men, balanced energy of female/male energy can create a healthy connection with their gentleness and strength. **A NOBLEMAN ... SO ATTRACTIVE IN A MAN ... VERY APPROACHABLE.**

A woman with an overpowering amount of male energy can come across as aggressive and controlling, creating fear in a relationship. A woman with a lot of female energy may act like a helpless little girl, using her femininity to get attention.

A man who is connected to a lot of his feminine energy and ignores his male energy may be in fear or lacking self-worth. High male energy in a man may be expressed as control, masking their lack of self-worth. This behavior may bring out fear in a relationship.

The balance between our male and female energy can be a barometer to the level of suppressed emotions and past history still living inside.

Our female energy can nurture and care for the sensitive heart and intimacy between two people. The male energy emerges as courage and strength, inspiring protection and change.

CHAPTER TWENTY-FIVE

Settling for Crumbs

Can you be brutally honest and ask for more from your partner and can you give more of yourself in a relationship? There needs to be give and take in the relationship to create a balance. Sometimes you need to give more and sometimes you need to receive more. Sometimes you need to support more and sometimes you need more support. It's about asking for what you need and not settling for crumbs. The crumbs you take may have been given out of a lack of awareness and if you settle, you are living in lack.

A true beloved relationship is worth striving for or leaving for. To inspire happiness by being happy and sharing this with another person creates a beloved relationship if the other person does the same. Your example of love and happiness and how you share yourself will come back to you. Be the example of what you desire, live it, ask for it and if you don't get it, leave for it.

The Shattering

Many things may shatter the relationship, such as money issues, career struggles and lack of intimacy, or illness and loss. Try not to blame, judge or abandon your partner. If you can hold the space, get clarity and work it out together, this experience can deepen the relationship.

See The Signs

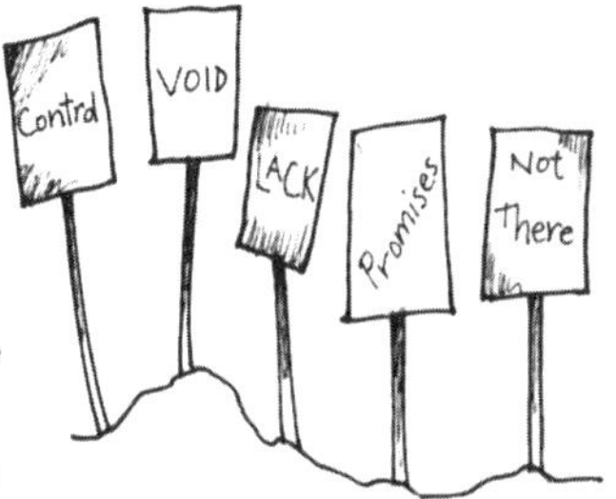

In the movie *Bruce Almighty*, Bruce says, "God, send me the signs, send me the signs." The signs, so clear to the audience, are not visible to Bruce. When we're awake in the relationship, we see and feel the signs of inauthenticity, lack of self-worth or suppressed issues. Signs of lack of love can be experienced in a relationship in so many ways.

Case Study: Sandra and Kevin
Issues: ***Letting go of an uncomfortable relationship***

Sandra had been in a relationship with an unavailable man for many years while she waited for the relationship to become a committed one. Kevin continued to disappoint her by not showing up or not taking the relationship to the next level. Sandra would get upset and cut it off until he wooed her back with promises. She would believe him instead of taking care of herself. The signs were there and Sandra could see them clearly, yet she refused to take them personally. Her forgiving nature and desire for Kevin's love was stronger than her love for herself.

Sandra spent most of the time waiting for Kevin to show up. By holding onto the dream of them together, Sandra gave Kevin the power and control over her love and peace.

She revisited this truth, becoming wiser and stronger, until she recognized the lack of love and became responsible for her life. Letting go of Kevin was a painful decision but Sandra began to heal her heart and her wounded past.

Our body signals are a big part of our wake-up call. We can feel the anxiety in our body when we are with someone we aren't comfortable with. When we don't feel like our natural self, our body is saying, "This is a dance where I don't feel good, so what's going on?"

Take a good look at this dance. If we are not safe to be all that we are, we can feel it when the other person merely breathes. We are all energy and if that same energy that makes us uncomfortable comes into our space, we can choose to listen to what our body says and honor the place in us that doesn't feel authentic. Can we say no to the relationship?

You can be present and awake as you get to know someone. Connect to what your body and your heart are feeling? Are you breathing fully? Are you comfortable in your skin? Do you feel open with this person?

You can't make someone love you. You can try, by repeatedly giving, being all you think you should be for them, but then you start to lose touch with yourself. Ask yourself – are you being all that you are, or everything they want you to be?

You cannot make anyone feel love but you can show up fully loving, respecting and taking care of yourself. Be aware of the signs in your life, in your body and listen to your heart.

It's not up to anyone to give you that love. It's for you to know that the love is in you and to feel it. Once you are in that place, which is the beloved space, if someone is meant to be with you, they will want to be with you because they are comfortable. In the beloved relationship you will feel respected and safe to be all that you are – even when you make a mistake – without being reprimanded, scolded or looked at with disapproval. Each partner is safe, feeling the opportunities of personal growth, independently and together.

It's not our responsibility to make anyone change or think the way we think. We can only inspire another person by our actions. Whether or not they want to take responsibility is up to them. Be present and awake; listen to your heart. It will never misguide you.

Partnership can be

Life or Death of our wounds

Life or Death of our spirit

CHAPTER TWENTY-SIX

Inner Peace

For me, God is another word for love. To be the love is touching the God within – the source of love, peace and strength. Inspire your life and your world with the love and peace within you.

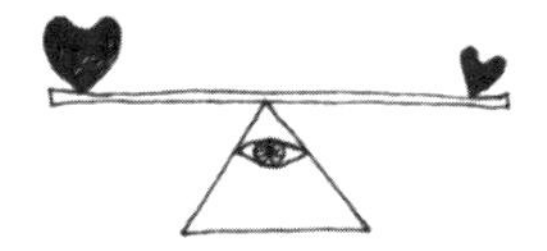

Balance

The light and the dark, the love and the pain – our understanding of our pain is as important as our love. The light of our life brings up the dark and the integration of ourselves becomes the one. When our perception has no fear and we have found a way to merge with both the light and the dark, the love and the pain, the miracle of this experience creates the vision of our future.

We must feel the pain in order to know the love. If we can feel our uncomfortable emotions connected to our past, we can live present in the space of peace.

Every tough relationship is as important as the easy ones. Each one brings us to a part of ourselves that needs to be experienced.

Balance ... Spirituality, Physical Exercise, Healthy Eating for your Mind, Body, Spirit

Can we love ourselves enough to create the personal balance of space for our spiritual practice, plus time for physical fitness, emotional fitness and healthy eating to nourish our bodies? It's important to bring the balance into our relationship, to inspire one another when imbalance is creating separation.

In a new relationship, the love (which is the light) will bring up our dark side, which is our past pain. When we feel a lot of love and the days together are wonderful, the recurrence of past pain needs to be felt, experienced and released. Some relationships never get past this stage because neither party wants to feel the discomfort the relationship creates. It's important to hold the space for one another so that we can get back into balance, re-connecting to the source of our own love.

When the romantic love is shattered, it's time for the Inner Workout and the re-connection to our own love and peace. This REAL love can create the intimate, safe experience to go deeper in the relationship.

Take care of your own mind, body and spirit and stay balanced.

Love Love Love ... Does It Feel Good or Yucky?

I believe that whether we want to admit it or not, love is the most powerful expression in our life.

Love has been woven into our lives and we only know it as we have experienced it. In fact, we really don't know how big it is until we get there. We have no way in this moment to know or measure love any deeper than how it once felt or didn't feel.

Movies, books, relationships and dreams can show us how we have not loved or how we have. Sometimes I wonder if it's love or the illusion and void that keeps us looking.

To some, the *language of love* is like a foreign language. How can we speak it, write about it or live it if we haven't experienced it? How do we know what we've experienced anyway! What are we all searching for?

I looked for love everywhere, in people and in things, in successes and accomplishments, in all the wrong places ... dark places. I thought I'd found love in different corners of the world ... and one day I finally found it and *it was inside me!*

Like the song "Love Is All Around You," we can't feel it unless we know it is in us. The heart is the symbol of love. Our physical heart is the connection to our survival ... *so is love.*

I experience many people who get turned off when it comes to romance. I also witness their heart shutting down as they begin to feel unworthy or hurt by the memories of love. We can react negatively to anything if it brings up our void, the lack of love or lack of self-worth connected to a personal experience.

Seeing belovedness around us can inspire us as we see examples in a tangible form, not just as dream or illusion. To experience it, know it in ourselves and see it in someone else can be a constant reminder of what we desire in our life.

People go to movies and read love stories because it evokes the feeling of love in them – the space to feel what they desire and hope for with love. Books and movies can also remind us of the darkness and the abuse, the separation and abandonment of relationship, which cause us to feel the pain that we may not have released yet. I hope this book will inspire you to create this desire within and to inspire your life as you examine the places relationships have taken you and the places it has not.

The love that you feel within is your own reflection. The book or movie just reminds you that it is in you. If you take care of your emotions and let go of your past with this formula, you'll find your way to that space you can be connected to. Eventually you won't need books or another person to bring it up for you, you'll recognize that it's in you. You'll live it and that's when you'll attract it. One day you won't settle for anything less than that.

The Beloved

(Meditation by Bruce Smith)

There is a place where each of us feels at peace, alive and free where our hearts shine and our eyes sparkle. Where we can expand our perception and feel the flow of energy from the universe course through every cell of our bodies. Where we connect from deep within and smile in our freedom.

From this place of our highest vibration, we are free to achieve everything that we are, to see our own purpose and to reach for the stars.

From this place, we feel our ultimate state of oneness. With ourselves we are free to love and honor the beauty within that the universe created in our souls, to inspire or mirror others to reach the place of higher vibration. To achieve in that moment, total freedom from the prison of the mind and from the fears and the heaviness that can weigh us down and slow our vibration to one of stress, or pain or unhappiness.

By learning to shed the heaviness of our anxieties and our fears we can restore our spirits to inner and outer beauty, peace and contentment.

From that place, we each can open our third eye so we can recognize our beloved when he or she steps into our life and the opportunity open for recognition by one of each other.

To smile, to feel a connection to the core of your soul to know that this is the one.

For if your own peace, love and freedom lies in achieving your own highest vibration, then your heart wants to be with the one who inspires you to exist in that place. To inspire in each other the path to healthy and deep fulfillment and to personal growth within a loving partnership.

The power of a beloved relationship will heal partners, friends, family and colleagues as they are each opened and drawn to their own places of higher vibration.

From that place, there is no anger, wounds or heaviness, only love and light. A gift for one, a beloved relationship in two. The path to knowing your own truth and the beauty we can each inspire.

The beloved relationship is found first from within. From that place of peace and light, it creates a safe place that will draw your beloved to you and will open you to recognizing your beloved from the first moment of connection.

CHAPTER TWENTY-SEVEN

The Goddess and The Nobleman

The Goddess is the female example of living the connection of inner love, self-worth, wisdom, peace and strength. The Nobleman is the male example of living the connection of inner love, peace, self-worth, wisdom, peace and strength. When the Goddess joins together with the Nobleman, they are already ignited and connected to their own fire and the passion moving through their bodies. *This is a powerful union.*

Step into the shoes of the Goddess or Nobleman and feel the parts of you that are woven within these words. Touch that part in you that holds you back from feeling open.

Who Is The Goddess?

The Goddess is connected to
her own natural beauty.
She allows her heart to be open.
Her energy is light and you feel
her strength and courage
in her silence.
You know her commitment in her eyes and
her inspiration in the truth in the way she is living.
She does not wear her pain for the world to see,
she takes care of it, yet she is not afraid to
share it without blame.
She is not afraid of the future as she lives
present in the moment.
She's connected to her life force, which unites
her passionate living and wisdom as she speaks.
You know the beautiful dreams are reality
because she's been there and has experienced it.
She has melted the armor around her heart,
feel the softness.
Her eyes see the magnificence of you
when she looks into your eyes.
She listens to you because the information that you are
sharing with her is important
and she hears you because she knows herself.
Her silence exudes acknowledgement of her presence in
the moment and her soul is giving you the
audience you deserve.
She recognizes your talents and lifts them up in her heart.
When you are with her you feel safe to be
all that you are.
She reveals herself to you as equal yet you know

that she is touching
the divinity within the Goddess that she is.
She does not have to convince anyone of anything
... she lives it.
Her authenticity creates a transparency and you
know that she lives from truth.
She trembles with you in her compassionate heart
as she believes in the healing of the moment.
Her wisdom comes from all the ages,
not from the intellect of the mind.
There are no shackles of control because she remembers
when she once was controlled. She is easy to be with
because she is comfortable with herself.
She will take you by the hand where you can remember
that you too
are a Goddess or a Nobleman.
We can recognize her because what we see in her is in us.
Remember the Goddess in you.

Who Is The Nobleman?

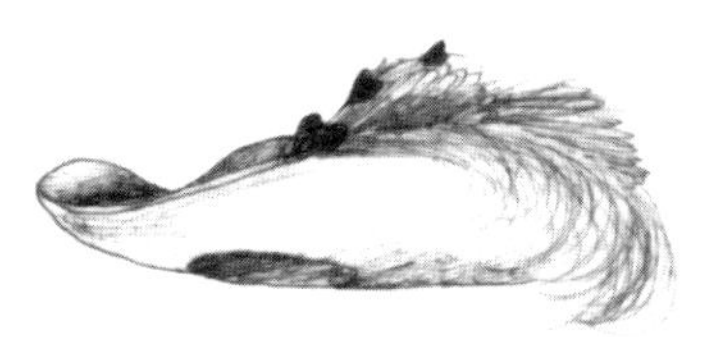

Can we open our hearts to the goodness of men who have chosen a partner and family to find out more about themselves? The Nobleman lives within each man and life can sometimes disconnect this truth. Each of us can forget the qualities of the Nobleman when we are disappointed or shut down. If we forget the inner truth, the following commentary may remind us of the brilliance of this connection, available to every man.

The Nobleman lives his manhood with gentleness and
quiet strength.
He creates a safe place for you to live and be inspired.
His eyes of love come from his connection deep within.
You can feel that he adores you as no other.
He is a brother to all of your friends,
and a loving father to all of the children.
He lifts your passion carefully in the beating of his heart
and he knows just when to take you to new places.
He is safe to be with because
he has created the safe waters.
He takes care of his own demons and fights
them to their death,
embracing them with his heart, and releasing
them to the heavens.
The Nobleman lives with his head and heart connected
and loves from his passion.
He knows peace because it lives inside him.
You know that he is a Nobleman because
when you look into his eyes you can see his soul.
He has no secrets, nothing to hide.
He walks with confidence because his self-worth is strong.
Remember the Nobleman. He lives in every man.

The Nobleman and Goddess reflect each other. Male and female energy take the lead when one or the other is needed. Each is both and one.

CHAPTER TWENTY-EIGHT

Communication

The language of love quietly embraces fear. No one is right or wrong. Some people process while they speak by expressing judgments or attachments and projecting emotionally, but this can cause the other person to shut down. Try to listen and feel so that you can do your inner processing before you speak. Sometimes people just speak to fill the silence, so take the time to breathe and feel before you communicate. Our body language communicates our hidden emotions. Take time to connect with the truth of what you really feel.

Beloved Language

The Beloved Language is honoring and respectful

Communication and intimacy are a huge part of the beloved experience in relationship. Sometimes the intensity of our emotions creates an opportunity to deepen a relationship. When we take care of our own anger we aren't afraid to speak truth. In the beloved relationship, we trust that we are not judged, so we are free to share anything. When we move together in the world, our beloved communication with our body language can inspire others. Our beloved energy is talking the same language. We are in alignment with our attitudes. People notice the difference because they feel the open heart of our relationship as we walk with the same truth.

People notice us because we are different than the majority of relationships in the world. The beloved relationship is an inspiration when others see the joy, the love and the closeness. To communicate this loving, beloved relationship is a gift that inspires other men and women to honor and respect one another.

I remember a day years ago when I was walking on the beach, feeling my desire for partnership. I looked over as the sun was setting and I saw a man and woman who had to be in their 90's, dressed in evening attire ... she was in a gown and he was in a tuxedo. As the sunset inflamed the beach and calmed the waters, this beautiful, beloved couple waltzed to their inner music. What a magical sight as I sat alone with my hope and watched them dance. They ignited my desire and I knew that was what I wanted ... to grow old with someone and dance on the beach of my life.

Many people have told me how they see Bruce and I in our relationship. They observe how we talk to each other with respect, how we look at each other, how we hold each other in an honoring space while one of us is talking or telling a story. We have an inspiring relationship and our communication and intimacy with one another is no different when we are alone or with others. We have no hidden agenda, no pretenses. Our relationship is authentic.

We constantly take care of our own issues and if we are out socially and issues come up, we re-connect within and try not to bring it into other people's space. We are seamless when together and our children, family and friends can feel our beloved relationship any time and any place. Our independence is attractive and we experience pride when one of us achieves or accomplishes something.

I have experienced relationships where issues and problems are discussed or projected in public with one person putting down the other. This is uncomfortable for all concerned. I remember communicating intimate issues because I didn't feel safe discussing them in private. That was my problem … I was afraid to speak up.

Some people like to share their garbage with others, not honoring the relationship or anyone else. Couples who argue in front of other people or are shut down with one another may not be taking care of their own issues in a healthy way. They usually don't know any other way. I have compassion for this because, in my past, I didn't know any other way either. My anger or resentment emerged when I least expected it or I'd complain to others instead of facing it myself. When there is drinking involved, the suppressed anger and judgment will frequently come out, posing as an excuse to be rude.

Take care of your resentments and fears so that you don't have to communicate them to everyone else. Honor your partner and create a safe place to deal with issues within your relationship.

Communication Leads To Intimacy

Stay involved with your relationship, ask questions, get clarity, talk about your desires and get to know each other at every stage of your life together. Communication is an evolving process creating more intimacy. Live with the desire to get to know the other person and let the other person get to know you. If one person stops being involved, separation occurs. Two people may be married or living together, but not in a committed partnership, so they're really not together.

Many people feel fear when the other person shuts down and they don't ask for clarity. Ask questions and develop a sense of safeness to talk with one another. If the other person doesn't answer you, make sure you ask why. You should feel respected and safe in an intimate relationship. Some women say, "He doesn't want to talk about himself, he doesn't share, he's just not interested in talking about it with me." They fear that by rocking the boat their partner will leave or won't support them anymore.

Go to your bridge and practice with your partner, face the fear of intimacy, speak the truth about your desire, feel the feelings, get to the pain and fear of it and detach from his/her being responsible for your fear. Bit by bit speak to your partner with your open heart, without resentment. You have to take care of the resentment living in you because of all the times he didn't listen to you or shut you out.

Getting to know each other at every stage in our life means remaining interested as we change and evolve. Check in on all aspects of your partner's life and be authentic. Genuinely feel that interest in one another. He wants to get to know ME. She wants to get to know ME.

When dating, understand what kind of intimacy and communication the other person has to offer, and if they don't share with you and they don't communicate, then you'll know that's their pattern. Don't settle for less just to keep the relationship. It won't thrive without communication or the safeness to be all that you are. Your relationship will shift and change, as will both of you if you take the time to communicate with one another once you are clear and connected within. It all starts with the inner relationship. Practice on the bridge and become an intimate partner.

Communication Exercise

Many couples don't listen to one another. They shut down and don't hear because they feel blamed, judged or criticized. If the other person feels like the victim and constantly whines and talks about the same thing over and over again, their method of communication can be very unappealing or threatening, especially if it's tied to blame and judgment. Taking care of your emotions and becoming more clear and staying in touch with the individual on an ongoing basis, without blame or judgment, is very, very important. Projection of resentment will cause guilt and your partner will shut down. Share yourself without control, blame or judgment.

I have an exercise that I use with my clients when they start learning about the process of communicating without blame, judgment or criticism. I have a private number that my clients can call anytime. I don't pick up on this line, but they know I will eventually listen to their messages. Whenever they have an issue or are triggered, they call and share their feelings. They practice communicating their experience with a person without blame, judgment or the projection of anger. They talk about what makes them feel angry or afraid. It's remarkable to hear people start to take responsibility for their feelings. As they leave their message, they feel their anger, re-connect with truth and then usually find a solution as they let go of the uncomfortable emotions.

This exercise provides a positive way to release and re-connect. You can use a tape recorder and do the same thing ... it's a great way to practice creating healthy communication. Eventually the client starts to talk about their feelings differently when they come to a session because they learn to do it from the place of self-acceptance and inner truth. If they are in relationship, usually their partner starts noticing the difference right away and they start feeling safer. What a fantastic experience, to inspire your partner with healthy communication.

YOU CAN'T TELL ANYONE HOW TO SPEAK OR HOW TO LIVE ... BUT YOU CAN INSPIRE THEM

Confrontation is communication filled with anger and resentment and may be embraced by judgment and blame. Sometimes we need to confront someone and our anger supports us in taking the steps to speak or stand up for ourself. When you take care of your heavy emotions, your words will be clear and your message has a chance to be heard. Practice with your Inner Workout it will keep your uncomfortable emotions moving through you. You can confront, blame, judge and feel your anger privately, on the imaginary bridge. You can then communicate with a lighter heart ... respecting yourself.

As we take care of our suppressed pain from past experiences and we take care of our emotions, we find more peace inside. This peace is always waiting to be felt and we are able to communicate in every aspect of our life without the dark energy that can shut down the lines of communication.

If someone needs to vent and project, it's your choice to be with them or not. Venting can be toxic in a relationship. Whining can also be annoying. Encourage the other person to talk about what they're feeling. You're not there to fix them but to hold the space. If someone starts venting or dumping, it's okay not to want this experience. Find an opening to give your opinion and leave the conversation. If someone is venting, you can share your feelings or opinion because they've opened the door for you. But when it gets tiresome or repetitive, take care of yourself and leave. Silence can be perceived as acceptance!

The need to be right is part of the male energy and the feeling of being wrong connects to our sensitive female side. The push and pull of right and wrong can take us to self-righteousness or self-doubt. Everyone has an opinion. It can be exhausting to try and convince someone they're wrong. Listen with an open heart so that you can hear what the other person is feeling or thinking. Honor their opinion, suggestion or information. You may not agree but that is what makes us all unique. Flexibility softly creates the space for intimacy.

TO BE HUMBLE HAS GREAT STRENGTH

The Face of Truth

I want to live with my connected, authentic self in relationship. My human nature is sometimes flawed but I do my best to find my way back to the connection that knows who I am.

I experience love deeply when I believe in myself. I experience fear deep within the core of who I am when I don't understand who I am in the moment, or who the other person is. So I need to take the time to find my way with my eyes open, to see what the issue is that separates me from my love.

I invited my dark side to show me what I needed to see and my relationships have shown them to me … the past that I needed to unveil, explore, accept, embrace and move with. The deeper I went, the more I saw. It was as if I had designed a pathway for myself, but realized later that the journey was created for me before I got here. Life can be complex when we look at the mystery of the unknown. If we realize that this plan, is for our soul's evolution, it's easier, it's softer, because we know that on the other side of this experience of struggle and pain, we can find more peace.

Intimacy

Create a safe place within the beloved relationship so that you can move deeply into your soul's lessons. Whatever your past is, whatever the damage or wounded pain is, hold a safe, open heart so that issues can be expressed and experienced. This safe place for intimate communication deepens and strengthens the beloved relationship.

Sometimes we may know the truth of our own plan and we hold back this truth to protect someone. If we speak with honesty, they may need to go to their pain or void so that they can heal. When we give them the opportunity to make their own choice instead of trying to protect them, we let go of control.

Try not to control your own emotions; give them a safe place to be felt.

Intimacy begins with you.

CHAPTER TWENTY-NINE

Beloved Passion

Passion is like a prayer, to feel the passion with your love … touch … lips. To surrender into the relationship and to be hungry for this love that is within. To be ignited and inflamed …to emerge into this place of you and me … this union where we become one.
To know that this will always be mine … this place that has no pain, this place that has no remembrance of past, only this moment of ecstasy. Two people meet in this beloved place not needing love from the other because they are connected to their own well of love within. Connecting in the presence, sparked together. Create an inner fire that is moving to embrace as you explode into the passion of divine love for all of eternity.

Take care of your past suppressed darkness, the wounds of abandoned love. Fill your own void and strengthen your own worth. Believe in yourself and the love that is yours and see in another all of their possibilities. Open your eyes and your heart to the freedom of Spirit and see your self as you look into their eyes. Feel your love when you are open to your heart. Listen to the language of the divine heavenly passion in the breath of each other. Take the time to lift your vibration each day to live the beloved experience with your partner.

Sexuality

Sexuality can be the ignition fired by safe love. Make love all day – it doesn't have to start in the bedroom. Holding, touching, being interested, complimenting, looking at each other with the eyes of love. Allow your soul to speak as you move, keeping your heart open. Duty will never be comfortable; faking it will always be felt. Create the safe place within each other's heart.

Spark the relationship with romance, sharing time, messages and the knowingness of commitment. Vibrate with passion ignited by you. The heart cannot inspire sexual energy if the heart is in fear, self-doubt or shut down. Hold the space for each other to move into safe love. Invite desire and spark each other with honesty, respect, tenderness, caring sensitivity and kindness.

Set the mood from the inside.
Let it be the reflection for the space outside of you.

Foreplay is creating the opening and

creating a safe place

but really

the **open heart** is foreplay

Admire each other

**I believe that when we are looking for our partner we are seeking the one who will not judge us, who knows us
because they know themselves.**

The Juicy Orange

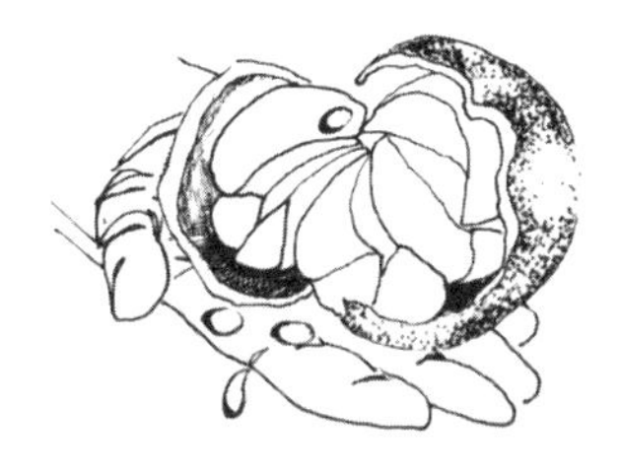

Sexuality and passion with the beloved is like an amazing, juicy orange. Two hands unfold the orange peel, as the juices invite you to experience the pleasure. Although I was never fond of oranges, twice in my life I have experienced a perfect, juicy orange and now I'm constantly searching for this orange, this experience, again … the one that's perfect and pleasurable for me.

I believe the experience of the juicy orange is like two people experiencing passion together.

When I think about the passionate, sensual experience with my husband Bruce, I see a vision of this juicy orange. I peel the thick orange skin of protection exposing a transparent skin that is so light and tender that the juices burst from the seedless flesh. The explosion of the sweet nectar of love tastes clear and full of flavor. The metaphor of the juicy orange helps illustrate the experience of safe, transparent love and passion intimately shared when the outer skin of protection and the open hearts between us ignite the flow of passion taking us to divine union.

When we are transparent with our own authenticity and our self-love, creating a comfortable, safe place with our partner, we are free to allow our passion for life and love ignite us and reflect in one another. For the Goddess to know her sacred feminine vibrations and for the Nobleman to be patient and create a safe place as she slowly unfolds herself, the Goddess will invite you in … trust and allow your gentleness to take you to the sacred union where you feel God … ALL THE LOVE THAT YOU ARE.

Take Back Your Sexuality

I have worked with many women and some men who say to me that they don't feel a connection to their sexuality or that it feels dead or shut down. I have also been in this place and realized my sexuality was still connected with a past experience or past lover. Self-worth and your connection to self-love play a big part in your sexuality.

When you have unresolved issues or suppressed emotions, it's hard to feel the connection to your open heart. It creates a barrier or lack of desire to be intimate with someone.

You might have left your sexuality with a past relationship. One woman felt shame with her first husband when they made love and she visualized the bridge and felt the shame with him, realizing that her father had made her feel bad about her sexuality, calling her loose when it wasn't true. She brought both her dad and ex-husband onto the bridge and felt her emotions, telling them how she felt. Then she took her sexuality back, feeling the connection in her as she re-connected with her Goddess self. Another woman felt she had left her sexuality with a past lover because the relationship was so loving and passionate. She too put this lover on the bridge and felt the void of love in her without him, taking back her sexuality.

One of my male clients felt considerable anguish about his sexuality and couldn't perform. He realized that once as a young male he was laughed at by a woman and this experience put such pressure on him, that he eventually rejected his own sexuality. He put the woman on the bridge and cried out loud and felt his humiliation. He felt his own sexuality emerge as he stopped making her responsible for his lack of desire.

Take back your sexuality and allow it to live fully in you.

Fall in Love ... over and over again.

Each stage of our self-growth and aging process
brings us to new levels of acceptance
of personal and physical changes.

Every stage is an opportunity to fall in love with
ourselves again.
Our bodies take us through change and our emotions
take us into acceptance.

Making Love

How can we create a comfortable relationship of intimacy? Creating the warmth in our own skin and the safeness as we melt into it is like being embraced in a warm bed by an electric blanket with a range of controls from low to high. We need to take care of the block that stops the energy that warms us and creates comfort.

If we can feel ourselves wrapped in our own arms, we have the power to switch on the inner furnace of love. Self-love is fueled by our desire to explode in every cell of our bodies and share it with another. For two people to join together with this fire, without being needy or manipulated, is wonderful, heart to heart, as your skin touches skin. As you feel the intensity of the openness that creates this heavenly place of inner happiness, feel each other's highest vibration and hear the sounds of peace embraced with trust and loyalty. You know it when you have arrived ... two souls uniting with the flame. Nothing else in this moment exists outside the fire of connection and conviction of the heart. From this place, ultimate divine love is inspired and felt in the rapture of the unconditional love.

I believe that foreplay is the preparation for making love all day long – making love within, being in love and sharing this place. It doesn't happen unless you are open to everything, to the safeness within and to each other.

How do we get there? For some, books and movies create this yearning. A lot of people have never experienced it in their life because they have not taken care of it for themselves. In the beloved relationship, it takes two, both being in the same place or inspiring each other.

My experience is that I cannot be in love when I am shut down. I cannot make love if my heart is closed or if I am thinking about the past or worrying about the future. How wonderful it is to have a partner who holds you in their arms as you share issues and talk about how you're feeling. Not expecting your partner to fix it, but to hold the space for you to express or feel. Start by creating the safeness in you and inspire the relationship. Commit to the one who is showing up and feel your own love with him/her.

Get to know this person intimately, because you have taken the time to know yourself. Inspire her or him; be the example of the connection to self-love.

They might never have had the safeness or experience to know how to be there. You won't know how to be there either if you don't practice your own connection to loving yourself. Be truthful with your feelings and prepare yourself. Fall in love inside yourself. Your mind, your body and your spirit are waiting to be united … create the mood in your home and with your physical body and your space. Candles and music create the energy that will help lift the vibration of your spirit. The longing to be here is every soul's desire and this is where we can heal. Take the time to touch each other's pain with your heart and without judgment. Embrace one another's darkness to find your way into inner safety. Allow your past and theirs to be present, so that you can know each other's darkness and not be afraid because it's hidden away or shut down.

Once we move into the rhythm of our heartbeat and feel the pleasure of the ultimate experience of union, this fullness will help release any tightness or holding back of the heart.

Don't fake it … if you cannot open yourself fully, don't pretend. This creates an experience that is not truthful. We have all been hurt and we all have fears. I believe a healthy, intimate union can continue to be healthy as long as each person takes care of their suppressed emotions. Supporting one another is not taking care of each other or fixing. Support is holding the space so that the safe passage through issues can result in an open, loving heart.

Everyone is searching for love and many move from person to person because the sexual ignition dies and they blame the other one when issues come up.

The experience of sexual ignition brings up the life force, which will move us into our heart to feel. If we are not prepared to go to our suppressed emotions, the experience can become overwhelming and we may want to run and hide. Be brave and stay to feel. You have a tool now to help you heal your wounded, damaged past.

You are worthy of love!

GOD MAKES NO MISTAKE IN BRINGING
TWO PEOPLE TOGETHER
TO FEEL TO LET GO TO HEAL

Many men do not know about love until they are making love. In this place they feel their heart. This can create a neediness to find it wherever they can, because it feels good. Many women, who are needy for love, take it in whatever way it's given to them. In one moment of ecstasy they feel their open heart and it feeds them and becomes an addiction.

Needy love and sex can become an addiction, because it may be the only place where we feel our passion or the openness.

Once you create the openness, safeness and passion that your life force can create, your sexuality and passion can always run through you. This energy is your fire, your passion for life and can keep you connected to your highest vibration. The power of your life force can give you strength and self-worth to overcome anything.

How we live in love is the love we know for ourselves. We are meant to have this every day of our life, not just a drop, or a notion of it. Love is vast and there is enough for all of us, not just for the chosen few. We are the ones who choose. We are the ones who have the power to choose it for ourselves and attract it and live in love with another.

I am told by some that it is rare. This is often the perception because people aren't aware. As more couples emerge into the beloved love to inspire the world, two by two, and inspire our children about healthy love, we can all become dancers with each other. Step by step, we will suddenly be a chorus line with beautiful music, and the stage of our own world will expand with others.

When we can ignite each other with our beloved light, one person at a time, two by two, eventually it will open to the masses. One day our children will know this beloved love and live it, teaching their children and so on. In the future the world will know this safe beloved relationship that started in you – the beautiful bliss we can feel in a relationship.

Make the choice to experience beloved, divine love, the result of the labor of love. There is work on our part; it's our responsibility and from this labor of self-acceptance, we can birth together the beloved experience.

The Connection

When you look at your beloved and know that you feel him in and around you, even when there is distance, he/she is in your heart, and under your skin. Even if you close your eyes, you know that he/she is there. You can feel the caress of their essence touching every cell of your being with gentle soft love. It doesn't matter where you are in a day, you can stop and feel that commitment and safeness of each other. Your loneliness doesn't exist anymore because you have already realized you are never alone. This place that exists within you is also in your beloved. When the time comes when you can physically touch one another, the joy catches fire in your heart, and the gentleness takes you home inside you.

Colleen Hoffman Smith

CHAPTER THIRTY

Conclusion

I believe that there are many different ways to love and feel the peace within our heart. Love can transform our life. We can become the alchemist, taking responsibility for our own life and changing within. I made changes within my relationships, understanding that I had free will.

Move on if the relationship is not acknowledged, respectful and growing. Our soul's evolution depends on us changing our perception. Melt into the places inside your heart that have shut down, so that you can live more of your soul's calling and desire.

Our heart has many pathways ... pathways to pain, to love and to future bliss ... and it is up to us not to block these pathways. Use this tool to open to a new beloved experience and the chance to be different ... feeling better than you did before.

As I sit here at our secluded cottage with snow burying us in, I can feel the beauty outside as the snow falls and the cold keeps us hibernated. In this moment I feel empty of all my attachments to my past. This book has been my own experience of the beloved and I sit here empty of judgment and blame for myself and all of the relationships with whom I have felt hurt and felt my darkness. Each experience has brought me to this place in me and I am so grateful to know the difference. Right now, in this moment, I am at peace.

Each thought ...

each feeling...

has come through me

and in the experience of it,

I know I am now choosing which way

I want to walk

and be in my life,

...and dance in relationship.

I choose us

The Beloved

Together within

Together hand in hand

LET'S WALTZ ON THE BEACH OF LIFE

The Beloved ... breathe it as you live with it,
tuck it in your heart and allow
the beloved relationship to find you.

Books, Music and Art that lifts my spirit and inspires my heart.

My triplet sister Frannie Hoffman, author of *From Modeling Clothes To Modeling Self,* takes you on a journey of remembering the simple truths of love. I encourage you to read her love story, it is a life changing experience. I am so proud of her and grateful that we came into this lifetime together.
www.franniehoffman.com.

My triplet sister Philomene Hoffman is a talented song writer and musician. Her music opens your heart as she takes you to the sacred mystery of life. Whether it is attending a live performance or spending some time listening to her latest recorded CD titled *Let Her Go*, my heart sings. I am so blessed to have her in my life. www.philomenehoffman.com

Nancy Newman's artistry and creative talent has brought joy to my life. Her soul portraits create a spiritual pathway from the wisdom of your soul. www.nanners.ca

Luke Andrews, my nephew, is a talented musician/songwriter.
www.lukeandrewsmusic.com.

Fred Napoli, author of *Re Inventing My Self.*
www.screenarts.com/Napoli/index.html

Yanka Van der Kolk, Imaging and Photography
www.powerofselfimage.com

Harvey Diamond, *Fit for Life*. www.harveydiamond.com

Robin Sharma, author of *The Monk Who Sold His Ferrari* and *The Saint The Surfer And The CEO.* www.robinsharma.com

Oriah Mountain Dreamer, author of *The Invitation*, *The Dance* and *The Call*

Darlene Montgomery author of *Conscious Women—Conscious Lives, Book I, Book II, and Dream Yourself Awake*

Patrick Ellis author of *Dying in Love* and *The Seven Journeys of the Soul*

Eckhart Tolle author of *The Power of Now*

Don Miguel Ruiz author of *The Four Agreements—The Series*

Louise Hay author of *Heal Your Body and You can Heal Your Life*

Cindy Stone author of *The Incidental Guru*

Paul Ferrini author of *Forbidden Fruit, Everyday Wisdom, Return to the Garden* and many more www.paulferrini.com

Marianne Williamson author of *Enchanted Love*, *Return to Love, A Woman's Worth*. www.marianne.com

Flo Calhoun author of *I Remember Union, The Story of Mary Magdalena*

Music I meditate with:

Sound Massage by Brigitte Hamm. www.hamm.meditation.de

AUM & OM by Lex Van Somerren www.somerren.de/

Secret Garden…the collection

About the Author

Colleen Hoffman Smith is an inspirational guide, facilitator and relationship expert. She lives in Toronto, Canada.

In her first book, *Pocket Guide to your He♥rt*, Colleen shared her unique process that transformed her life inspiring her readers to become more authentic, attractive and comfortable in theirs. She believes that we can all attract a life of love and peace when we find it within.

Colleen's formula has been the connection to her Inner Relationship, Inner Workout and Inner Peace. This process has strengthened her self-worth and self-love, allowing her to experience her life and relationships with an open and loving heart.

Pocket Guide to your He♥rt for Relationships has been her personal process to become the beloved and attract her beloved husband Bruce.

Colleen continues to inspire others to connect to that part in themselves to attract and inspire their beloved experience.

We want to hear from you.

Colleen would love to hear how
Pocket Guide to your He♥rt for Relationships
has inspired you in your personal and
professional relationships.
Please e-mail your comments to:
edentrilogy@rogers.com

To order books in quantity or if you would like
to have one sent to a friend, visit our website at:
www.pocketguidetoyourheart.com

Colleen is available for
Keynotes, Seminars and Personal Coaching
and also new for 2005:

LEADERSHIP

Feeling Good In the Workplace

Workshops Seminars Keynotes

Co-Create Your Program!

For further information please contact:
Jo-Anne Cutler at JC Connections
905-569-8334
pocketguide@jcconnections.ca

or visit www.pocketguidetoyourheart.com